1960s

Ten Years of Popular SHEET MUSIC BESTSELLERS

PIANO · VOCAL · CHORDS

THE HITS!

DECADE by DECADE

Alfred Music Publishing Co., Inc.
16320 Roscoe Blvd., Suite 100
P.O. Box 10003
Van Nuys, CA 91410-0003

alfred.com

Copyright © MMIX by Alfred Music Publishing Co., Inc.
All rights reserved. Printed in USA.

ISBN-10: 0-7390-6022-8
ISBN-13: 978-0-7390-6022-3

Cover photo: © istockphoto / genekrebs

Contents

Title	Artist or Show	Page
96 Tears	? and the Mysterians	4
All Along the Watchtower	Jimi Hendrix	12
Aquarius / Let the Sunshine In	The 5th Dimension	18
The Ballad of Gilligan's Isle	*Gilligan's Island*	24
Batman Theme	*Batman*	27
Blowin' in the Wind	Bob Dylan	30
Both Sides Now	Joni Mitchell	33
A Change Is Gonna Come	Sam Cooke	36
Dream a Little Dream of Me	The Mamas and the Papas	40
Everyday People	Sly and the Family Stone	43
(Meet) The Flintstones	*The Flintstones*	94
For What It's Worth	Buffalo Springfield	46
Gimme Some Lovin'	Spencer Davis Group	50
Gloria	Them	54
(Your Love Keeps Lifting Me) Higher and Higher	Jackie Wilson	62
Hit the Road Jack	Ray Charles	57
Hot Fun in the Summertime	Sly and the Family Stone	66
It's My Party	Lesley Gore	74
The Jetsons (Main Theme)	*The Jetsons*	71
Leaving on a Jet Plane	Peter, Paul and Mary	76
Like a Rolling Stone	Bob Dylan	80
The Lion Sleeps Tonight	The Tokens	85
Mack the Knife	Bobby Darin	120
Mama Told Me (Not to Come)	Three Dog Night	88
The Monster Mash	Bobby "Boris" Pickett	98
Mustang Sally	Wilson Pickett	104
Na Na Hey Hey Kiss Him Goodbye	Steam	108

Title	Artist	Page
The Night They Drove Old Dixie Down	The Band	110
One	Three Dog Night	114
People	Barbra Streisand	127
People Get Ready	The Impressions	130
Piece of My Heart	Big Brother and the Holding Company	136
The Pink Panther	Henry Mancini and His Orchestra	142
Puff the Magic Dragon	Peter, Paul and Mary	133
Raindrops Keep Fallin' on My Head	B.J. Thomas	146
Save the Last Dance for Me	The Drifters	150
She's a Rainbow	The Rolling Stones	154
Soul Man	Sam and Dave	160
The Sound of Silence	Simon and Garfunkel	164
Theme from A Summer Place	Percy Faith and His Orchestra	170
Sunny Afternoon	The Kinks	174
Sunshine of Your Love	Cream	178
Sweet Soul Music	Arthur Conley	182
Take Five	The Dave Brubeck Quartet	190
The Weight	The Band	187
What a Wonderful World	Louis Armstrong	198
What'd I Say	Ray Charles	202
When a Man Loves a Woman	Percy Sledge	214
A Whiter Shade of Pale	Procol Harum	236
Wipe Out	The Surfaris	218
(What a) Wonderful World	Sam Cooke	194
You Can't Always Get What You Want	The Rolling Stones	220
You Don't Have to Say You Love Me	Dusty Springfield	230

96 TEARS

Words and Music by
RUDY MARTINEZ

Moderate surf beat ♩ = 120

Verse:

Too man-y tear-drops for one heart to be cry-in'. Too man-y tear-drops for one heart to car-ry on.___

© 1966 (Renewed) ABKCO MUSIC, INC., 85 Fifth Avenue, New York, NY 10003
All Rights Reserved

You're way on top now, since you left me. You're always laughin' way down at me. But watch out now; I'm gonna get there.

C7
G
C7
We'll be to - geth - er
for just a lit-tle while.
G
C7
G
And then I'm gon-na put you
C7
G
C7
way down here.
And you'll start cry -
G
C7
G
in'
nine - ty - six tears.

C7
G
C7
Cry,
cry.
G
C7
Bridge:
Em
And when the sun comes up,
I'll be on top.
You'll be right down there
look-in' up.
And I might wave,
"Come up here."
But I don't see you

wav-in' now.
I'm way down here
won-d'rin' how
I'm gon-na get you.
But I know now
C
G
C7
I'll just cry,
cry,
I'll just cry.
G
C7
Too man-y tear - drops
for one heart

Lyrics:
to be cryin'. Too many teardrops for one heart to carry on. You're gonna

Chorus:
cry ninety-six tears. You're gonna cry ninety-six tears. You're gonna cry, cry, cry, cry now. You're gonna

G
C7
cry, cry, cry, cry nine - ty - six tears.
G
C7
Come on, let me hear you cry now nine - ty - six tears.
G
C7
Whoo! I wan - na hear you cry night and day,
G
C7
G
yeah, all night long, nine - ty - six tears. Cry, cry, cry,

C7
G
come on, ba - by, let me hear you cry now, all night long,
C7
G
a - nine - ty - six tears. Yeah! Come on now,
C7
G
a - nine - ty - six tears.
C7
G
C7
Repeat and fade

ALL ALONG THE WATCHTOWER

Words and Music by
BOB DYLAN

Moderate rock ♩ = 112

Verse 1:

1. "There must be some kind of way outta here," said the joker to the thief.

* Original recording: all guitars tuned down a 1/2 step in Cm.

All Along the Watchtower - 6 - 1

© 1968 (Renewed) DWARF MUSIC
Used by Permission of MUSIC SALES CORPORATION (ASCAP)
All Rights Reserved

A B C♯m B A B
"There's too much con - fu - sion,
C♯m B A B C♯m B
I can't get no re - lief."
Bus - 'ness - men they, ah ah,
A B C♯m B A B
drink my wine.
Plow - men dig my earth.
C♯m B A B C♯m B
None of them a - long the line
know what an - y of it is worth.

Verse 2:
A B C♯m B A B
Hey hey. 2. "No rea-son to get ex-cit-ed,"
C♯m B A B C♯m B
the thief, he kind-ly spoke. "There are man-y here a-mong
A B C♯m B A B
us who feel that life is but a joke. But uh,
C♯m B A B
but you and I, we've been through that, but uh,

C♯m B A B C♯m B
and this is not our fate.
So let us not talk false-
A B C♯m B A B
ly now.
The hour's gettin' late."
Hey.
3. Well
Verse 3:
C♯m B A B C♯m B
all along the watch-tower,
princess kept the view,
A B C♯m B A B
while all the women came and went,

C♯m B A B C♯m B
bare-foot ser-vants, too.
Well, ah oh, out-side in the cold
A B C♯m B A B
dis-tance, uh, a wild-cat did growl.
C♯m B A B C♯m B
Two rid-ers were ap-proach-in' and the wind be-gan to howl.
A B C♯m B A B
Hey.
Ah.

All Along the Watchtower - 6 - 6

AQUARIUS/LET THE SUNSHINE IN

Words by
JAMES RADO and
GEROME RAGNI

Music by
GALT MacDERMOT

Moderately bright (♩ = 184)

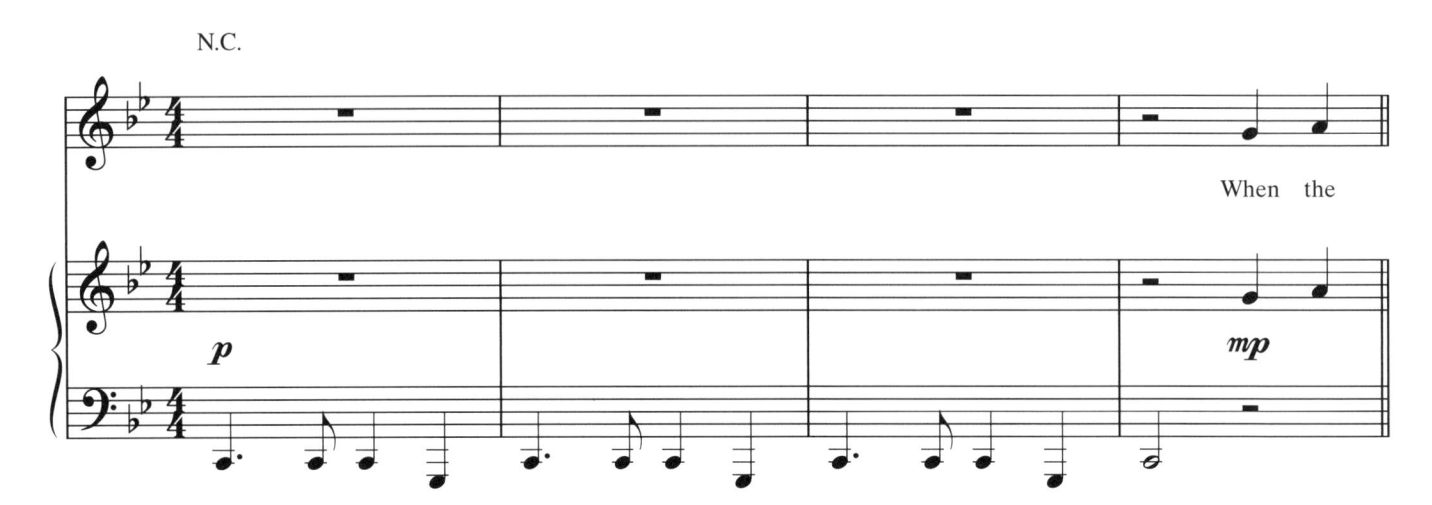

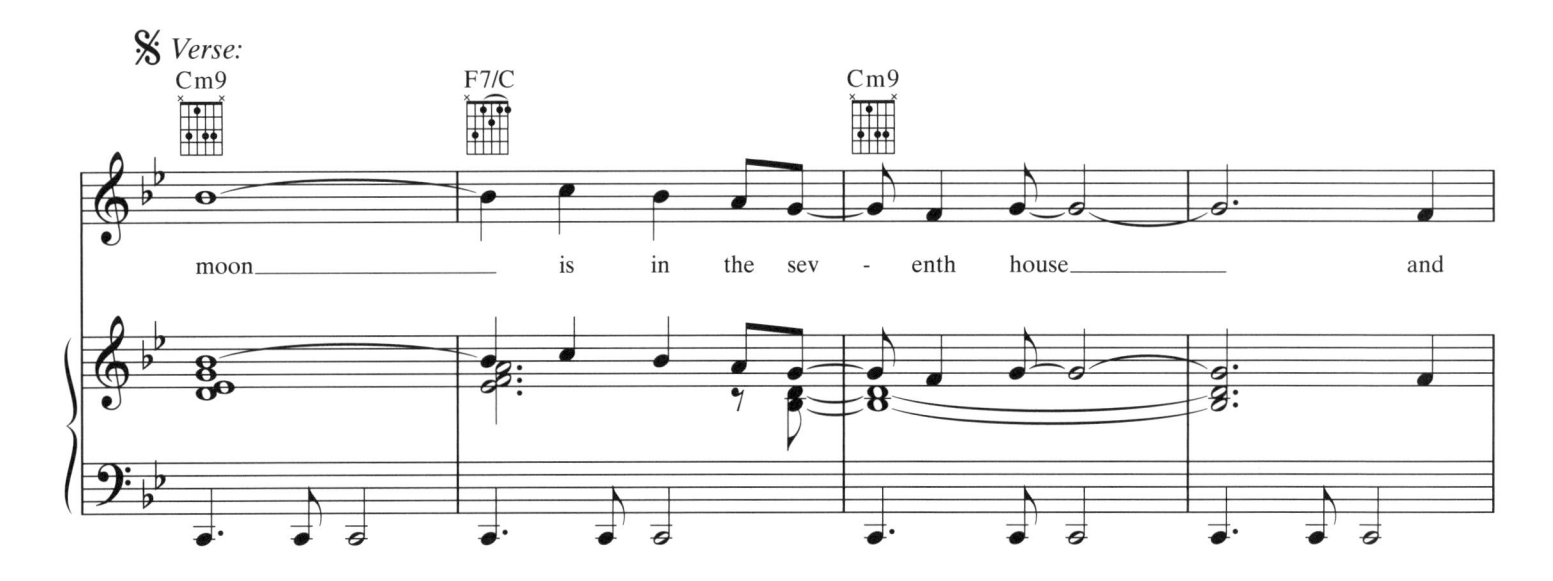

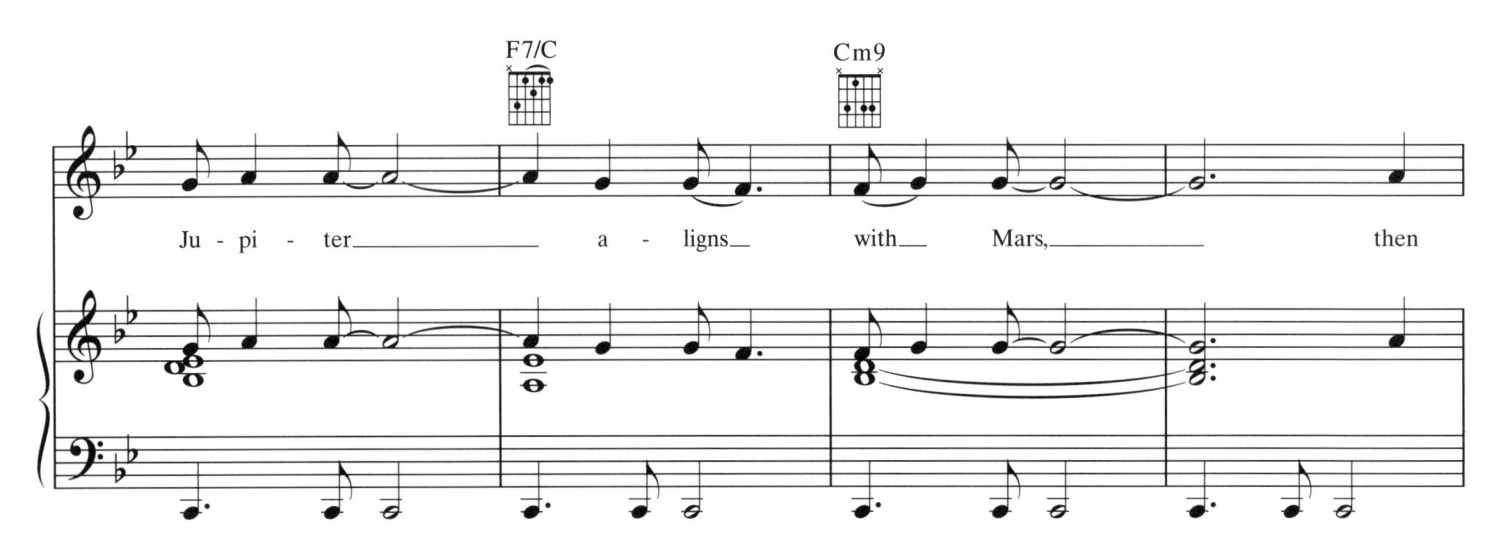

When the

Verse:
moon _____ is in the sev-enth house _____ and Ju-pi-ter _____ a-ligns _____ with _____ Mars, _____ then

Aquarius/Let the Sunshine In - 6 - 1

© 1966, 1967, 1968, 1970 (Copyrights Renewed) JAMES RADO, GEROME RAGNI, GALT MACDERMOT, NAT SHAPIRO and EMI U CATALOG, INC.
All Rights Administered by EMI U CATALOG, INC. (Publishing) and ALFRED PUBLISHING CO., INC. (Print)
All Rights Reserved

peace___ will guide_ the_ plan-ets___ and love___ will steer the stars.___ This is the dawn-ing of the

Chorus:

age of A-quar-i-us,___ age of A-quar-i-us.___ A-quar-i-us.___

Cm
A - quar - i - us.
To Coda
Bridge:
B♭7
E♭
Har - mo - ny and un - der - stand - ing,
f
B♭7
E♭
B♭7
sym - pa - thy and trust a - bound - ing.
No more false - hoods or de - ri -
E♭
Cm
G7/D
E♭
G7/D
sions, gold - en liv - ing dreams of vi - sions, mys - tic crys - tal rev - e - la -

Cm Cm7 Fm Gm
tion, and the mind's true lib - er - a - tion. A -
Fm
quar - i - us. A -
Cm
quar - i - us.
p
Cm9 Cm Cm9 Cm
D.S. 𝄋 al Coda
N.C.
When the
mp

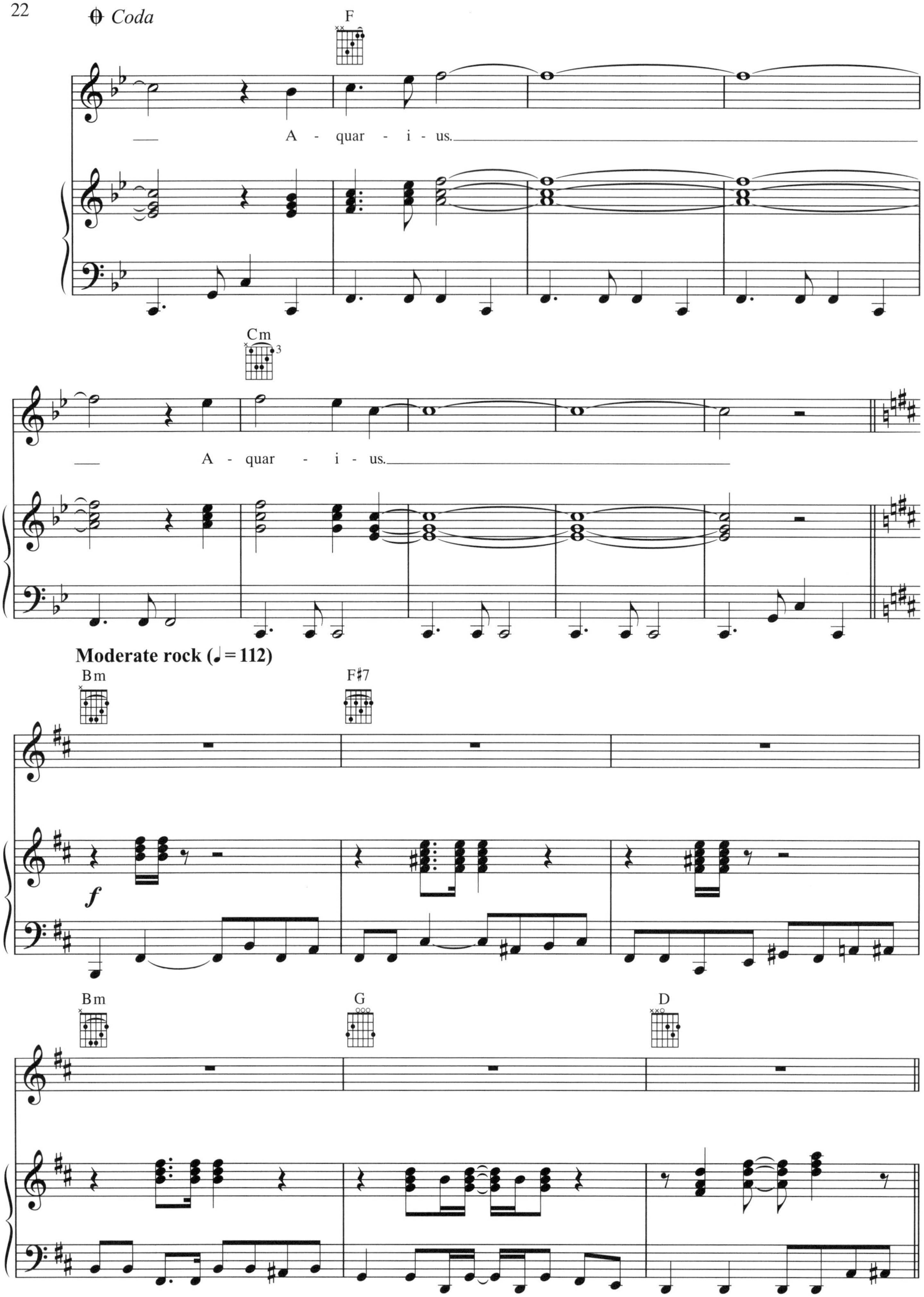
Coda
F
A - quar - i - us.
Cm
A - quar - i - us.
Moderate rock (♩ = 112)
Bm
F♯7
f
Bm
G
D

Bm
F♯7
Let the sun - shine.
Let the sun -
f–ff
Bm
G
D
shine in, the sun - shine in.
Bm
F♯7
Let the sun - shine.
Let the sun -
Bm
G
D
Repeat and fade
shine in, the sun - shine in.

THE BALLAD OF GILLIGAN'S ISLE

Words and Music by
SHERWOOD SCHWARTZ
and GEORGE WYLE

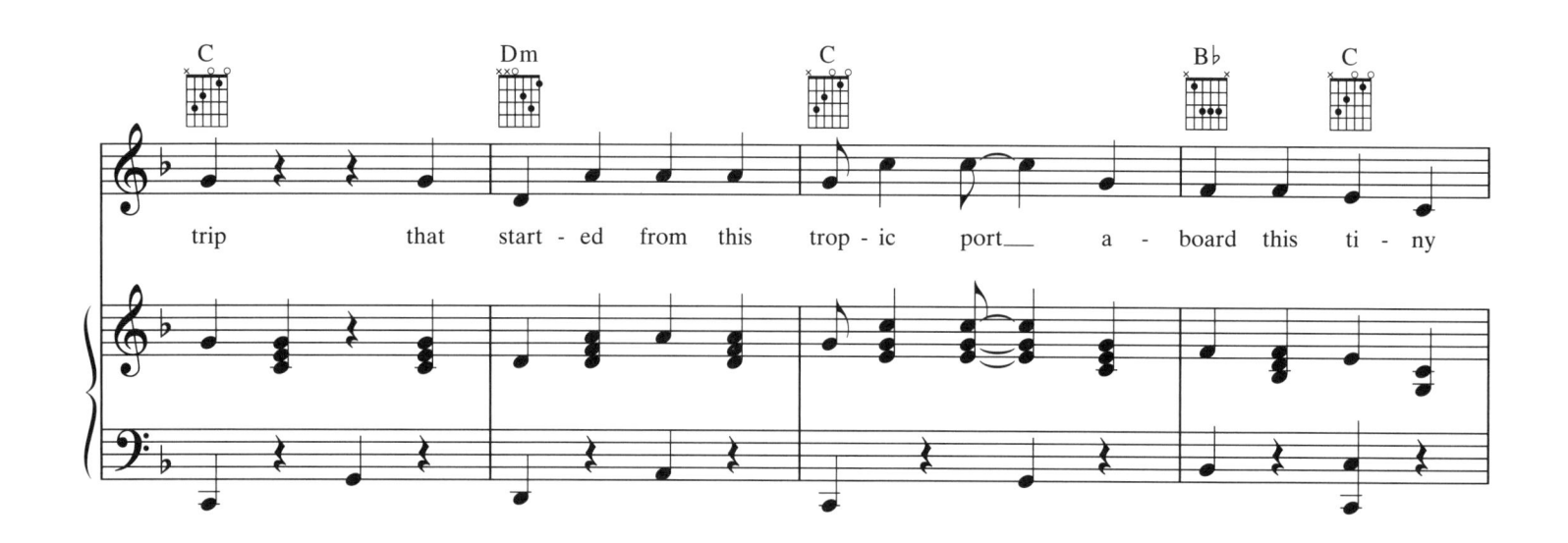

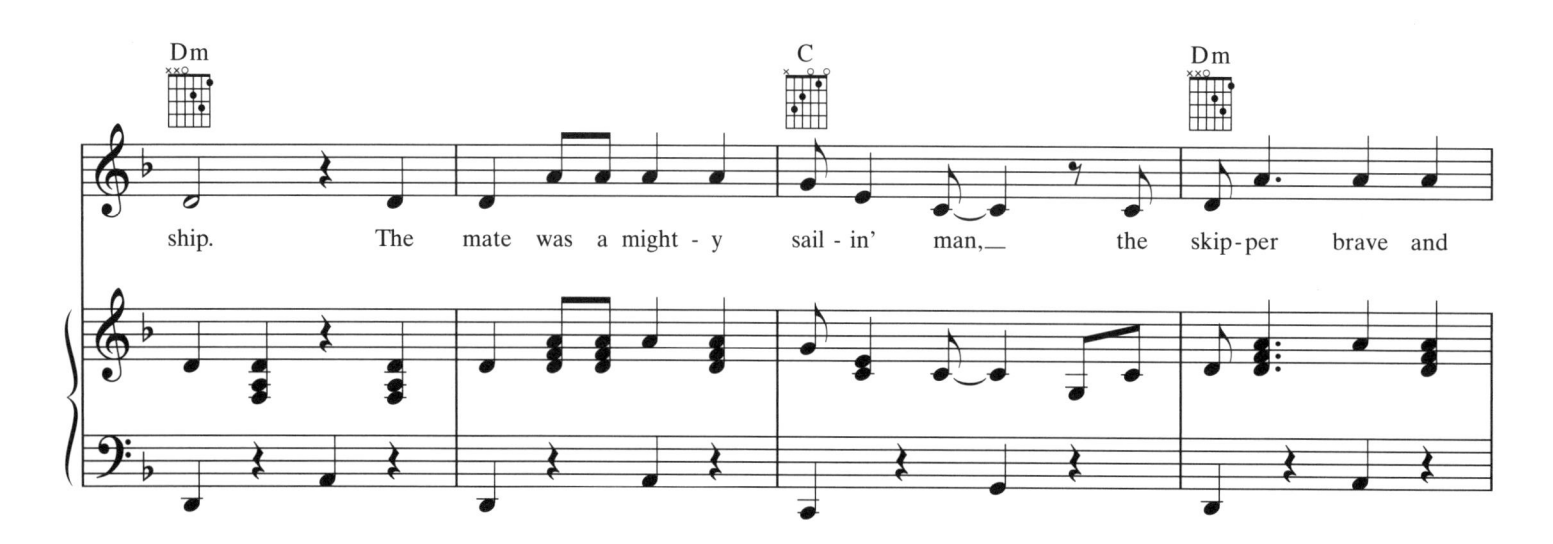

Lively

Just sit right back and you'll hear a tale, a tale of a fateful trip that started from this tropic port aboard this tiny ship. The mate was a mighty sailin' man, the skipper brave and

The Ballad of Gilligan's Isle - 3 - 1

© 1964, 1966 (Copyrights Renewed) EMI U CATALOG INC.
All Rights Controlled by EMI U CATALOG INC. (Publishing) and ALFRED PUBLISHING CO., INC. (Print)
All Rights Reserved

BATMAN THEME

Words and Music by
NEAL HEFTI

Bat Rock tempo (♩=150)

Batman Theme - 3 - 2

29

Batman Theme - 3 - 3

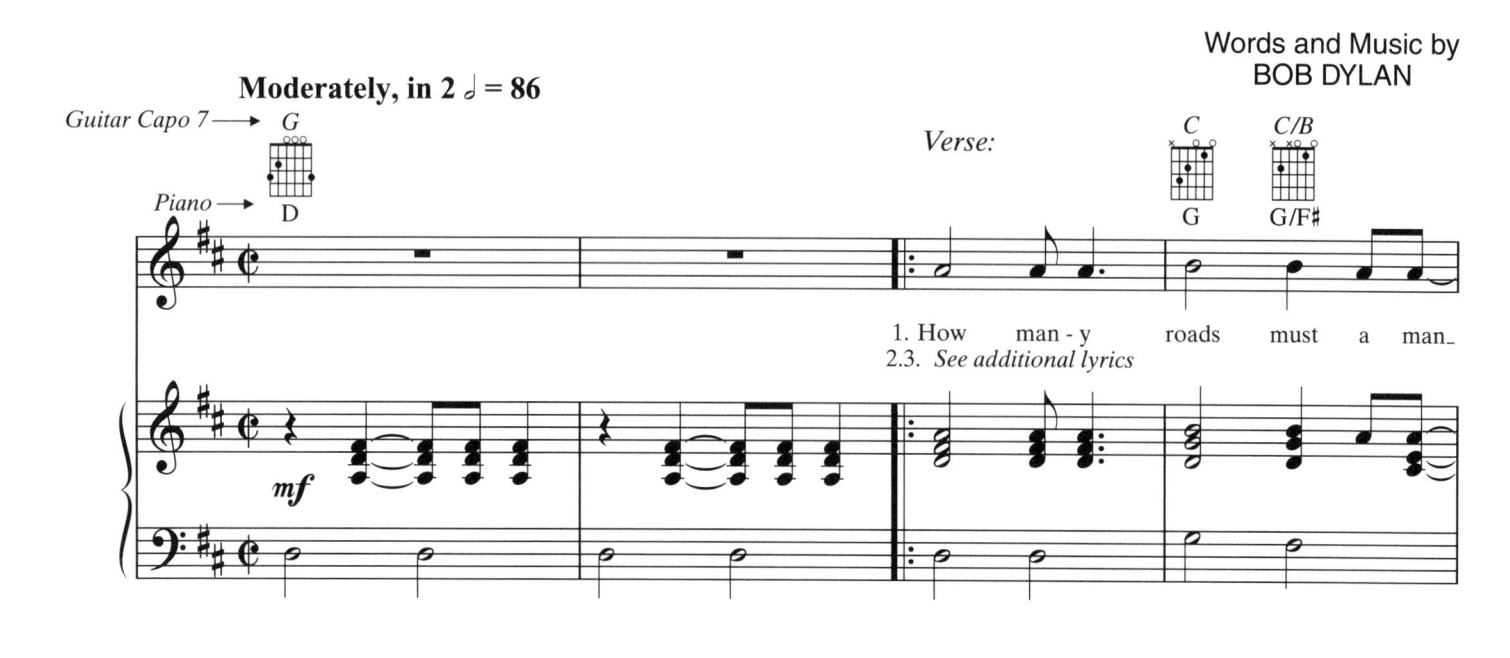

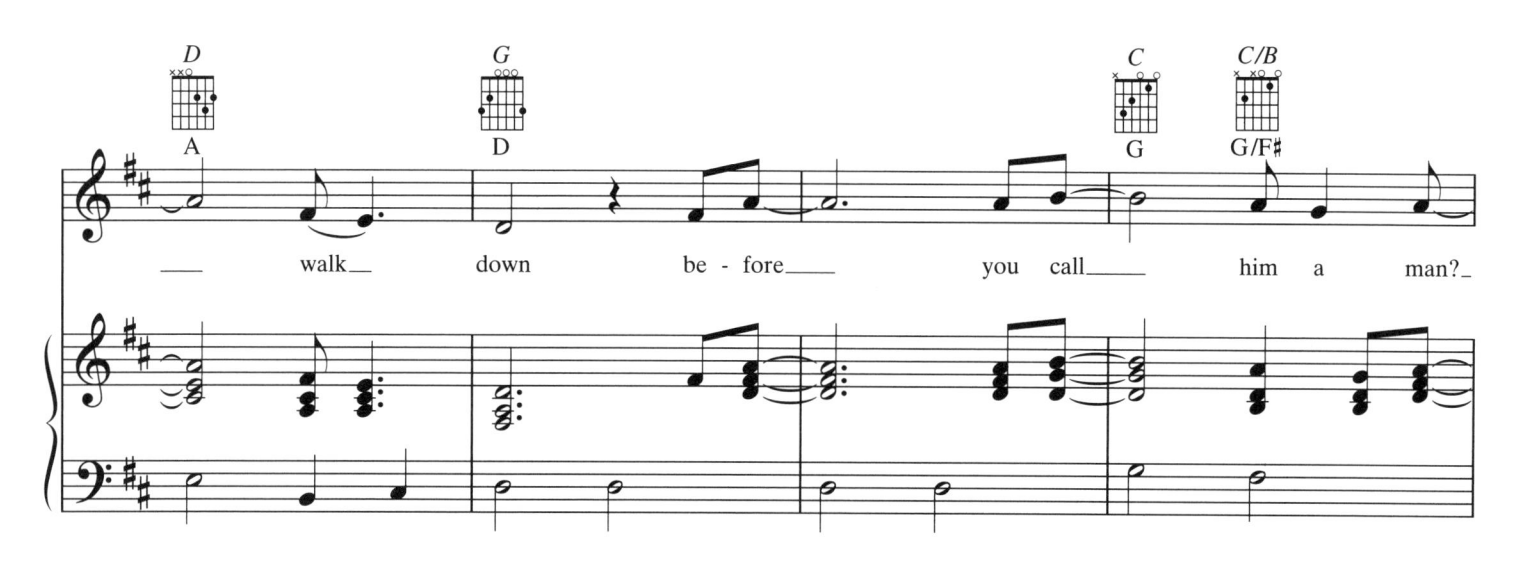

BLOWIN' IN THE WIND

Words and Music by
BOB DYLAN

Moderately, in 2 ♩ = 86

1. How many roads must a man walk down before you call him a man?
2.3. *See additional lyrics*

How many seas must the white

Blowin' in the Wind - 3 - 1

© 1962 (Renewed) SPECIAL RIDER MUSIC
Used by Permission of MUSIC SALES CORPORATION (ASCAP)
All Rights Reserved

dove___ sail___ be-fore___ she sleeps in the sand?___

Yes, and how___ man-y times___ must the can-

non-balls___ fly___ be-fore___ they're for - ev - er banned?___

Chorus:
The an - swer, my friend,___ is

Verse 2:
Yes, and how many years can a mountain exist
Before it is washed to the sea?
Yes, and how many years can some people exist
Before they're allowed to be free?
Yes, and how many times can a man turn his head
And pretend that he just doesn't see?
(To Chorus:)

Verse 3:
Yes, and how many times must a man look up
Before he can see the sky?
Yes, and how many ears must one man have
Before he can hear people cry?
Yes, and how many deaths will it take till he knows
That too many people have died?
(To Chorus:)

BOTH SIDES NOW

Words and Music by
JONI MITCHELL

Moderately ♩ = 112

Verse:

1. Bows and flows of an-gel hair and ice-cream cas-tles
2. Moons and Junes and Fer-ris wheels, the diz-zy danc-ing
3. *See additional lyrics*

in the air,____ and feath-er____ can-yons____ ev-'ry-where,
way you feel, as ev-'ry____ fair-y tale comes____ real,

Both Sides Now - 3 - 1

© 1967 (Renewed) CRAZY CROW MUSIC
All Rights Administered by SONY/ATV MUSIC PUBLISHING, 8 Music Square West, Nashville, TN 37203
All Rights Reserved

Fmaj7 B♭/F F2 Fmaj7 F6
I've looked at clouds that way. But now they on - ly
I've looked at love that way. But now it's just an -
F F6 F C/F C7/F F Fmaj7 B♭/F
block the sun, they rain and snow on ev - 'ry - one. So man - y things I
oth - er show, you leave 'em laugh - ing when you go. And if you care,
Fmaj7 B♭/F F2
would have done, but clouds got in my way.
don't let them know, don't give your - self a - way.
Chorus:
F Gm7/F F
I've looked at clouds from both sides now, from up and down, and
I've looked at love from both sides now, from give and take, and

Verse 3:
Tears and fears and feeling proud,
To say "I Love You," right out loud,
Dreams and schemes and circus crowds,
I've looked at life that way.
But now old friends are acting strange,
They shake their heads, they say I've changed.
Well, something's lost, but something's gained
In living every day.

Chorus 3:
I've looked at life from both sides now,
From win and lose, and still somehow,
It's life's illusions I recall,
I really don't know life at all.

Chorus 4:
I've looked at life from both sides now,
From up and down, and still somehow,
It's life's illusions I recall,
I really don't know life at all.

A Change Is Gonna Come

Words and Music by
SAM COOKE

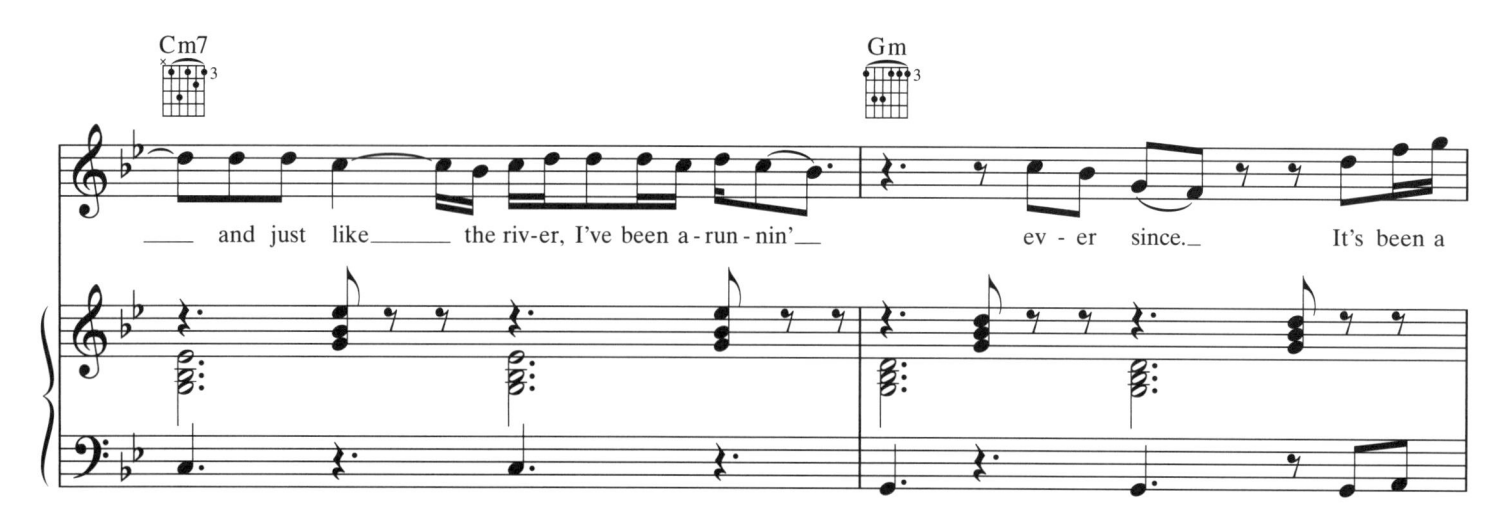

B♭
Cm7
E♭7
D7
long, a long time com-in', but I know, oh-oo-oh, a
Gm
1.
B♭
change gon' come, oh yes, it will. 2. It's been
2.
B♭
Verses 3 & 4:
B♭
yes, it will. 3. I go to the mov - ie and I
4. See additional lyrics
Cm7
go down - town. Some-bod-y keep tell-in' me don't

Gm
B♭
hang a - round. It's been a long, a long
To Coda
Cm7
E♭7
D7
Gm
time com-ing, but I know, oh-oo-oh, a change gon' come, oh
Bridge:
B♭
Cm7
yes, it will. Then I go, oh-oo-oh, to my
B♭6
Cm7
brother and I say, broth - er, help me

Verse 2:
It's been too hard living but I'm afraid to die
'Cause I don't know what's up there beyond the sky.
It's been a long, a long time comin',
But I know, oh-oo-oh,
A change gonna come, oh yes, it will.

Verse 4:
There've been times that I thought
I couldn't last for long
But now I think I'm able to carry on
It's been a long, a long time comin',
but I know, oh-oo-oh, a change gonna come, oh yes, it will.

DREAM A LITTLE DREAM OF ME

Lyrics by
GUS KAHN

Music by
FABIAN ANDRE and WILBUR SCHWANDT

Moderately

Refrain:

Stars shining bright a-bove you, night breez-es seem to whis-per, "I love you," birds sing-ing in the syc-a-more tree, dream a lit-tle dream of me.

Dream a Little Dream of Me - 3 - 1

© 1931 (Renewed) GILBERT KEYES MUSIC, WORDS AND MUSIC, INC., DON SWAN PUBLICATIONS and ESSEX MUSIC, INC.
All Rights for GILBERT KEYES MUSIC Administered by WB MUSIC CORP.
All Rights Reserved

Say "night-ie-night" and kiss me. Just hold me tight and tell me you'll miss me. While I'm a-lone and blue as can be, dream a lit-tle dream of me. Stars fad-ing, but I lin-ger on, dear, still crav-ing your kiss; I'm long-ing to

B♭7
E♭
D
D7sus
D7
lin - ger till dawn, dear, just say - ing this:
G
E♭7
D7
G
Sweet dreams till sun-beams find you, sweet dreams that leave all
E7
Bm7(♭5)
E7
Am
Am7
Am7(♭5)
wor - ries be - hind you, but in your dreams, what - ev - er they be,
1.
2.
G
Cm7
D7
G
E♭7
D7
G
dream a lit - tle dream of me.
me.

EVERYDAY PEOPLE

Words and Music by
SYLVESTER STEWART

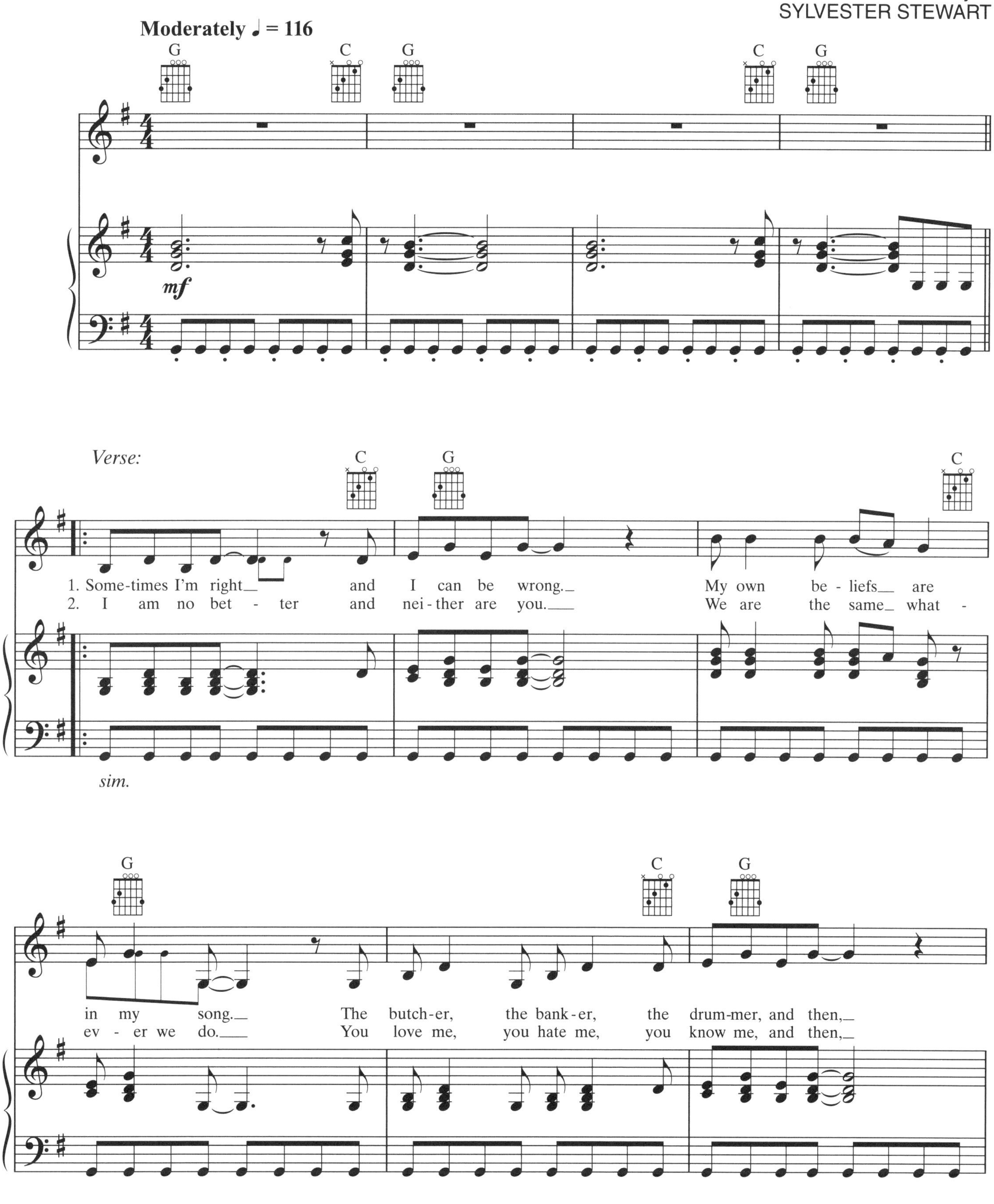

makes no dif-f'rence what group I'm in.
you can't fig-ure out the bag I'm in.
I am ev-'ry-day peo-ple, yeah, yeah.

There is a blue one who can't ac-cept the green one for liv-ing with a fat one, try'n' to be a skin-ny one.
There is a long-hair that does-n't like the short-hair for be-ing such a rich one that will not help the poor one.
There is a yel-low one that won't ac-cept the black one that won't ac-cept the red one that won't ac-cept the white one.

And dif-f'rent strokes for dif-f'rent folks. And

45

To Coda ⊕

so on, and so on, and scoo-bee doo-bee doo - bee. (Oo, sha sha.)

D.S. 𝄋 al Coda

1. We got to live__ to-geth - er.__
2. er.__

⊕ *Coda*

sha.__) I__ am ev - 'ry - day__ peo - ple.__

Everyday People - 3 - 3

FOR WHAT IT'S WORTH

Words and Music by
STEPHEN STILLS

Moderately slow ♩ = 98

Verses 1 & 2:

1. There's some-thing hap-pen-ing here, ____ what it
2. There's bat-tle lines be-ing drawn. ____ No-bod-y's

is ain't ex-act-ly clear. ____ There's a
right if ev-'ry-bod-y's wrong.

man with a gun o-ver there ____ tell-in'
Young peo-ple speak-in' their minds, ____ get-tin'

For What It's Worth - 4 - 1

© 1967 (Renewed) COTILLION MUSIC INC., TEN EAST MUSIC, SPRINGALO TOONES and RICHIE FURAY MUSIC
All Rights Administered by WARNER-TAMERLANE PUBLISHING CORP.
All Rights Reserved

me I got to be - ware.____ I think it's time we
so much re - sis - tance from be - hind. I think it's time we

Chorus:

stop, chil - dren, what's that sound?___ Ev - 'ry - bod - y look what's go - in' down._____
stop, hey,___ what's that sound?___ Ev - 'ry - bod - y look what's go - in' down._____

1. E A E A

2. E A

Verses 3 & 4:

3. What a field day for the heat; a thousand people in the street. Sing-in' songs and car-ry-in' signs, mostly say, "Hoo-ray for our side." It's time we

4. Par-a-noi-a strikes deep. In-to your life it will creep. It starts when you're al-ways a-fraid. Step out of line, the man come and take you a-way. We bet-ter

Chorus:

stop, hey, what's that sound? Ev-'ry-bod-y look what's go-in' down.
stop, hey, what's that sound?

Ev-'ry-bod-y look what's go-in'. You better

Repeat ad lib. and fade

stop. Hey, what's that sound? Ev-'ry-bod-y look what's go-in' down.

GIMME SOME LOVIN'

Words and Music by
STEVE WINWOOD, MUFF WINWOOD
and SPENCER DAVIS

Moderately fast ♩ = 148

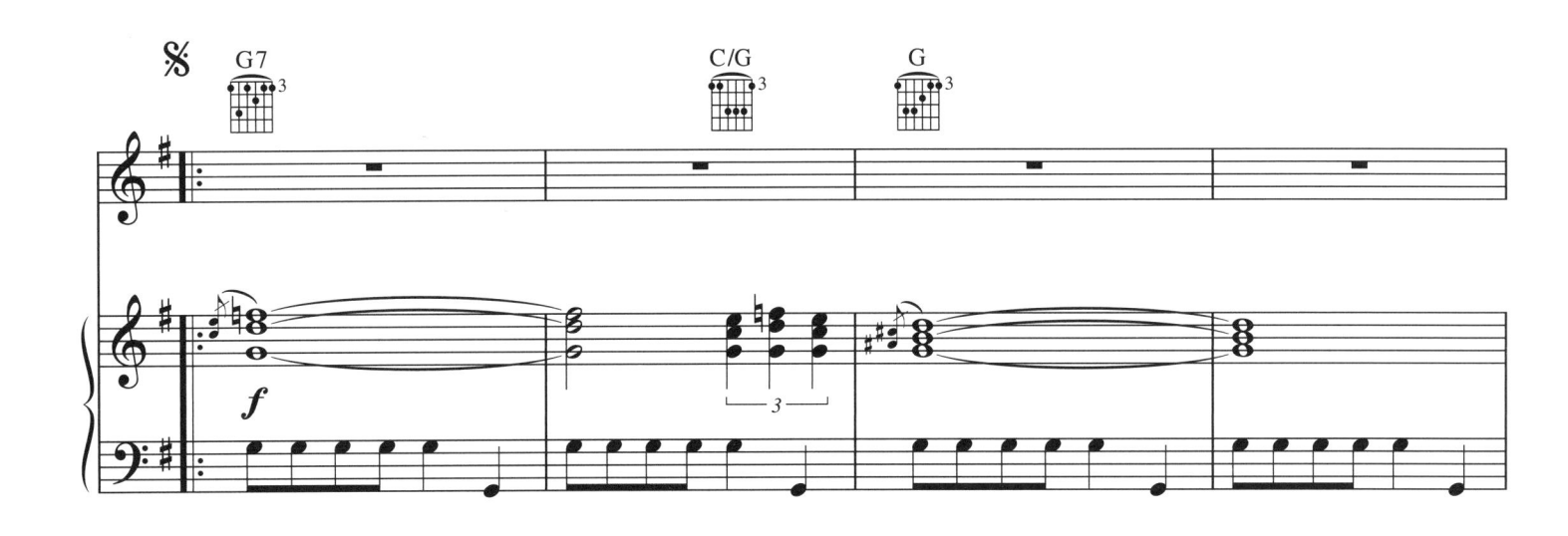

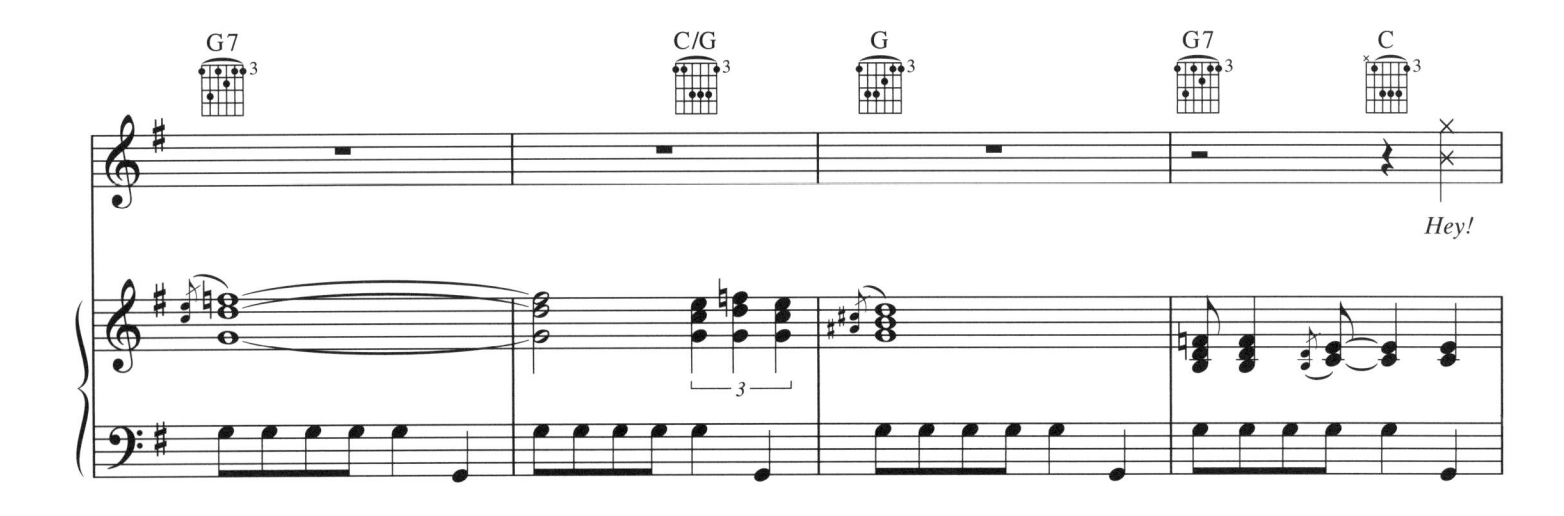

© 1966 (Renewed) F.S. MUSIC LTD. and UNIVERSAL–SONGS OF POLYGRAM INTERNATIONAL, INC.
All Rights for F.S. MUSIC LTD. Administered by WARNER-TAMERLANE PUBLISHING CORP.
All Rights Reserved

Verse:
G C G C G C
1. Well, my tem - per-'ture's ris - in' and my
2.3. See additional lyrics
G C G C G C
feet on the floor.__ Twen - ty peo - ple knock - in' 'cause they want - ing some more.__
G C G C G C
Let me in, ba - by, I don't know what you've got, but you'd bet - ter take it eas - y, this
G C G B♭
place is hot. And I'm so glad__ we made__ it,

Chorus:
C
E♭
G
so glad__ we made__ it. You got - ta
gim - me some a - lov -
C
G
C
in', (Gim - me, gim - me some lov - in'.) gim - me some a - lov - in', (Gim - me, gim - me some
To Coda
G
C
1.
N.C.
lov - in'.) gim - me some a - lov - in' ev - er - y day.__
2.
D.S. al Coda
N.C.
day,__ hey.____

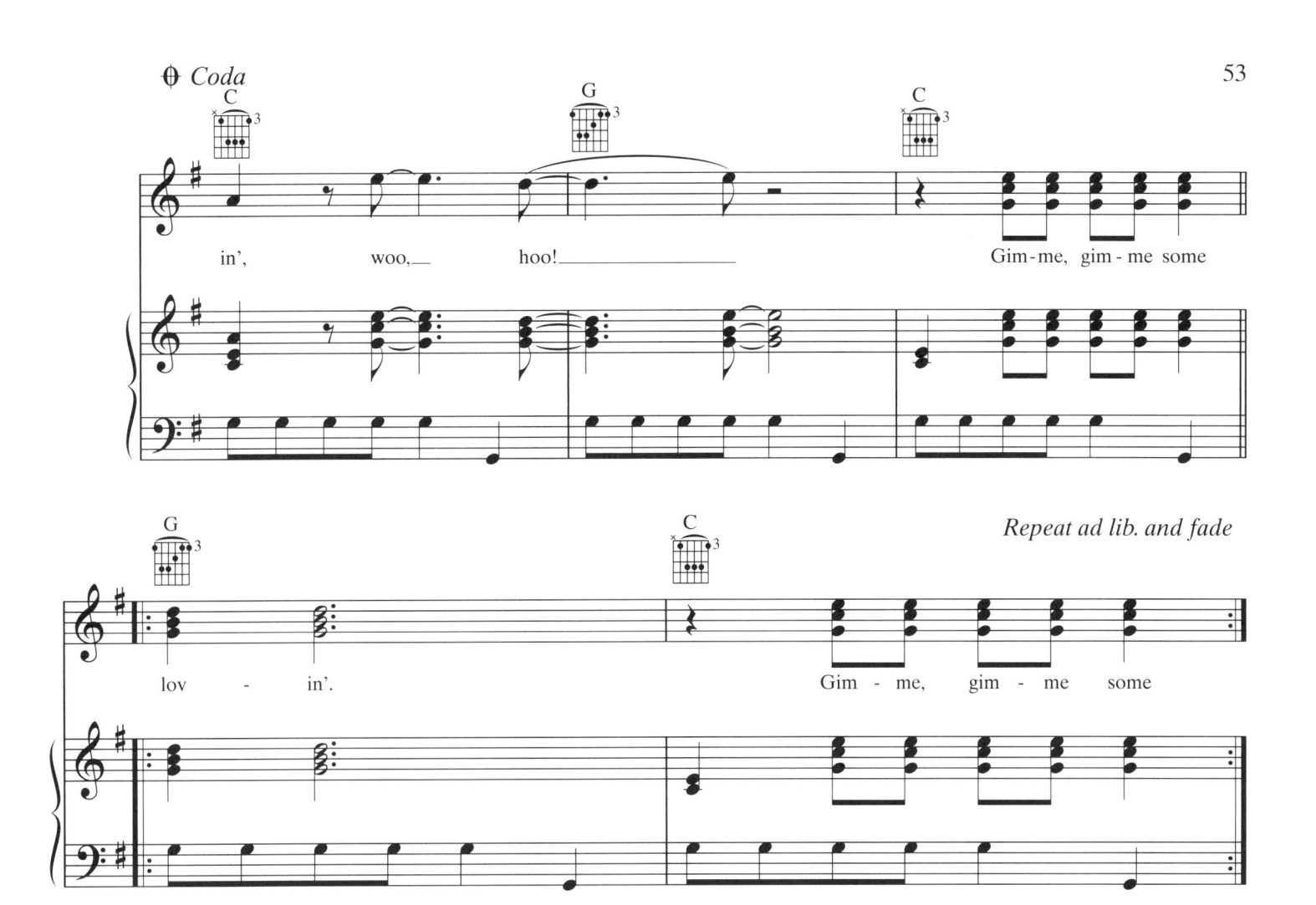

Verse 2:
Well, I feel so good, everything is sounding hot.
You better take it easy 'cause the place is on fire.
Been a hard day and I don't know what to do.
Wait a minute, baby, it could happen to you.
And I'm so glad we made it, so glad we made it.
(To Chorus:)

Verse 3:
Well, I feel so good, everybody's gettin' high.
You better take it easy 'cause the place is on fire.
Been a hard day, nothing went too good.
Now I'm gonna relax, honey, everybody should.
And I'm so glad we made it, so glad we made it.
(To Chorus:)

GLORIA

Steady rock ♩ = 120

Words and Music by
VAN MORRISON

Verse:

1. Like to tell you 'bout my ba-by. You know she comes 'round here, just a-bout mid-night.

just 'bout five feet four from her head to the ground.
Makes me feel so good, Lord, makes me feel al-right.

Well, she comes a-round here just a-bout mid-
Walk-in' down my street, comes up to my

Gloria - 3 - 1

© 1965 (Renewed) Unichappell Music, Inc. and Bernice Music, Inc.
All Rights Administered by Unichappell Music, Inc.
All Rights Reserved

night. She makes me feel so good, Lord, makes me feel al-
house. She knocks up-on my door, makes me feel al-

Chorus:

right.
right. Her name is G - l -

o - r - i - a.

G - l - o - r - i - a. G - l - o - r - i -
Glo - ri - a.

a. G-l-o-ri-a. Glo-ri-a. Glo-ri-

Al-right, one time. Glo-ri-a. Glo-ri-

a.

2. Yeah, she comes a-round

HIT THE ROAD JACK

Words and Music by
PERCY MAYFIELD

Moderately fast ♩ = 172

*N.C.

Chorus:

road, Jack, and don't you come back no more, no more, no more, no more. Hit the

road, Jack, and don't you come back no more. What you say? Hit the

*Original recording in A♭ minor.
Hit the Road Jack - 5 - 1

© 1961 (Renewed) TANGERINE MUSIC CORP.
All Rights Reserved   Used by Permission

Am F E7 Am F E7
road, Jack, and don't you come back no more, no more, no more, no more. Hit the
F E7 Am
road, Jack, and don't you come back no more.
1. Whoa,
Verse 1:
F E7 Am F E7
woman, oh, woman, don't treat me so mean. You're the meanest old woman that I've ever seen. I
Am E7 Am
guess if you said so, I'd have to pack my things and go. That's right! Hit the

Chorus:
F E7 Am F E7
road, Jack, and don't you come back no more, no more, no more, no more. Hit the
Am F E7 Am E7
road, Jack, and don't you come back no more. What you say? Hit the
Am F E7 Am F E7
road, Jack, and don't you come back no more, no more, no more, no more. Hit the
Am F E7 Am
road, Jack, and don't you come back no more.
2. Now,

Verse 2:

baby, listen, baby, don't ya treat me this a-way, 'cause I'll be back on my feet some-day. Don't care if you do, 'cause it's un-der-stood;_ you ain't got no_ mon-ey, you just ain't no good. Well, I guess if a-you say so, I'll have to pack my things and_ go. That's right! Hit the

Chorus:

road,_ Jack, and don't you come_ back no more, no more, no more, no more. Hit the

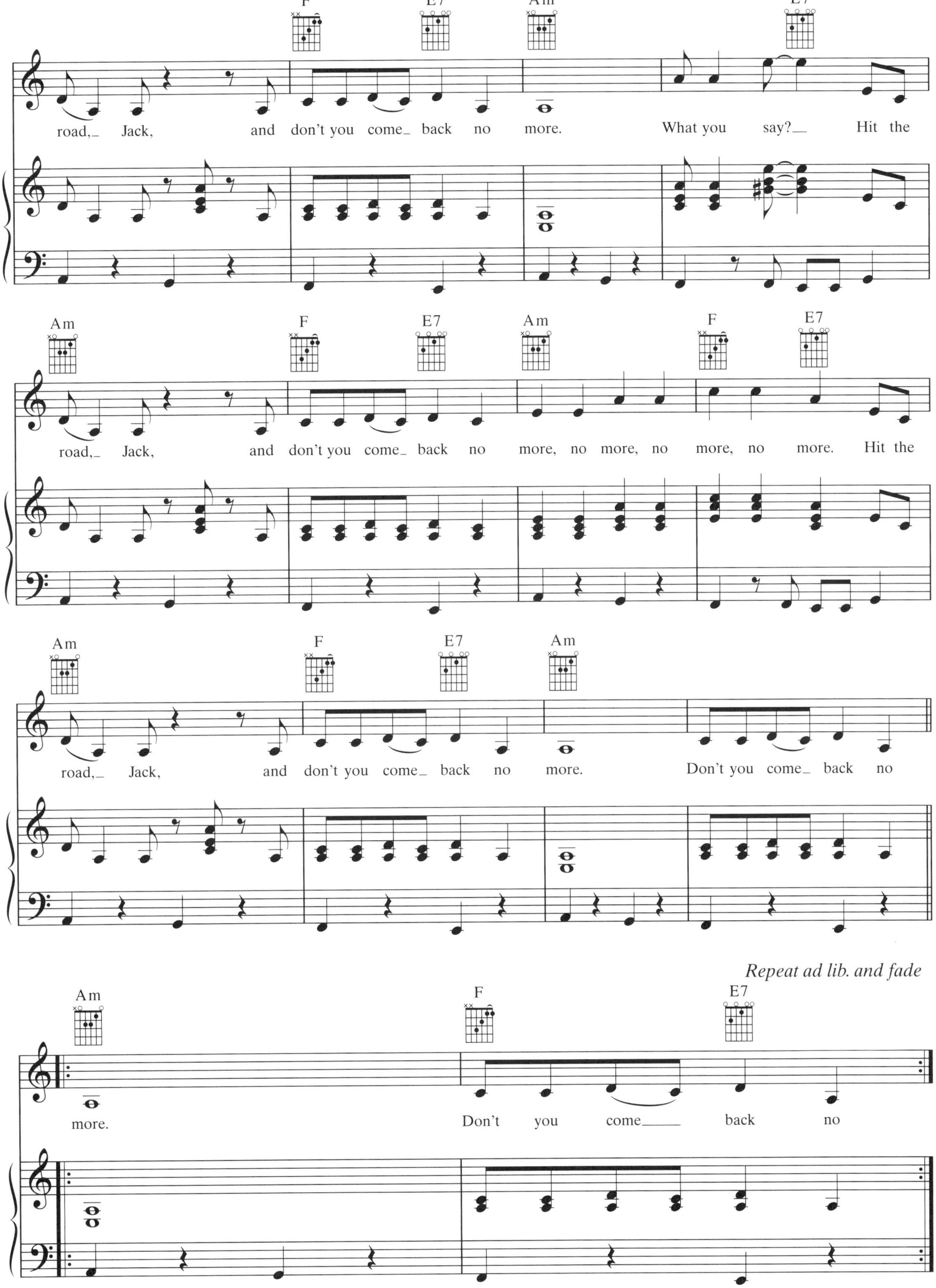

(YOUR LOVE KEEPS LIFTING ME) HIGHER AND HIGHER

Words and Music by
GARY JACKSON, CARL SMITH
and RAYNARD MINER

So keep it up,   quench my de-sire,
But then you came and he soon de-part-ed,
And now with my lov-ing arms a-round you,

and I'll be at your side for-ev-er-more.
and, you know, he nev-er showed his face a-gain.
hon-ey, I can stand up and face the world.

Chorus:

You know your love
That's why your love
Your love

keep on lift-ing me high-er, high-er and high-er.

(Your Love Keeps Lifting Me) Higher and Higher - 4 - 2

G
3
I said, your love keep on
Em
3
D
To Coda
lift - ing me high - er and high - er.
1.
2.
D
2. Now, once
G
3
Em
3

D
G
Em
D
D.S. 𝄋 al Coda
𝄌 Coda
3. I'm so
I said, your love
G
Em
keep on lift - ing me high - er,
D
Repeat ad lib. and fade
high - er and high - er.
I said, your love

HOT FUN IN THE SUMMERTIME

Words and Music by
SYLVESTER STEWART

Moderately ♩. = 96

Verse 1:

1. End of the spring ___ and ___ here ___ she ___ comes ___ back. Hi, hi, hi,

Hot Fun in the Summertime - 5 - 1

© 1969 (Renewed) MIJAC MUSIC
All Rights Administered by WARNER-TAMERLANE PUBLISHING CORP.
All Rights Reserved

E♭
hi there.
Them
Dm7
G7
summer days,
those summer days.
Dm7
C/E
F
Am
G7
Dm7/G
C/G
F/G
Verses 2 & 3:
C
Gm9
2. That's when I had most of my fun
3. First of the fall and there she goes

Hot Fun in the Summertime - 5 - 3

Dm7
C/E
F
Am
G7
N.C.
to.
want to.
Out of school,
county fair in the coun-
try sun,
and ev-'ry-thing is
cool,
ooh, yeah.
To Coda
F♯m7(♭5)
G
G/G♯
G/A
Em7(4)

Chorus:
Dm7 C/E F Am G7
Hot fun in the sum - mer - time.
Hot fun in the sum - mer - time.
Hot fun in the sum - mer - time.
Dm7 C/E F F♯m7(♭5) G7
D.S. 𝄋 al Coda
Hot fun in the sum - mer - time.
Coda
Repeat and fade
Hot fun in the sum - mer - time.

THE JETSONS (MAIN THEME)

Words and Music by
WILLIAM HANNA, JOSEPH BARBERA
and HOYT CURTIN

Jane, his wife.

Daugh-ter Ju-dy.

His boy El-roy.

73

(Spoken:) And

Ro - sy, the ro - bot maid.

The Jetsons (Main Theme) - 3 - 3

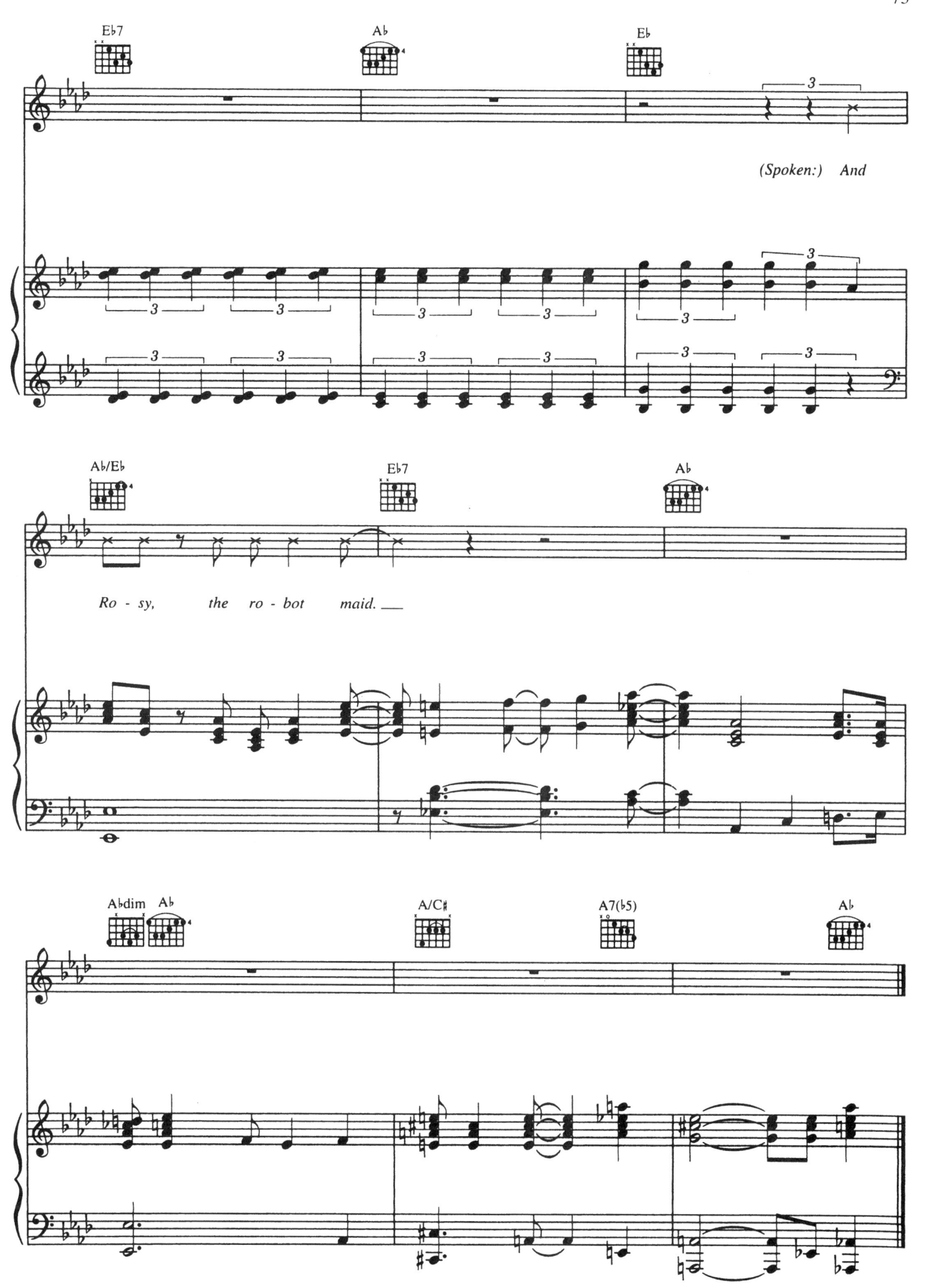

IT'S MY PARTY

Words and Music by
HERB WIENER, JOHN GLUCK
and WALLY GOLD

Moderately bright

holding her hand, when he's sup-posed to be mine?
danc-ing with me, I've got no, rea-son to smile.
birth-day sur-prise, Ju-dy's wear-ing his ring.

It's my par-ty, and I'll cry if I want to, Cry if I want to, Cry if I want to, You would cry, too, if it hap-pened to you.

LEAVING ON A JET PLANE

Words and Music by
JOHN DENVER

Moderately, with a light shuffle feel ♩ = 132

Verse:

1. All my bags are packed, I'm ready to go, I'm standing here out-
2. man-y times I've let you down, so man-y times I've
3. Now the time has come to leave you; one more time let

© 1967 (Renewed) CHERRY LANE MUSIC PUBLISHING COMPANY, INC. (ASCAP) and FSMGI (IMRO)
All Rights Controlled and Administered jointly by CHERRY LANE MUSIC PUBLISHING COMPANY, INC. and STATE ONE SONGS AMERICA (ASCAP)
All Rights Reserved

Leaving on a Jet Plane

Chorus:
A
D
So kiss me and smile for me,
A
D
A
Bm
tell me that you'll wait for me; hold me like you'll nev - er let me
E7
A
D
go. I'm a - leav - in' on a jet plane,
1. 2.
A
D/A
A
C♯m
I don't know when I'll be back a - gain; oh, babe, I hate

Leaving on a Jet Plane

LIKE A ROLLING STONE

Words and Music by
BOB DYLAN

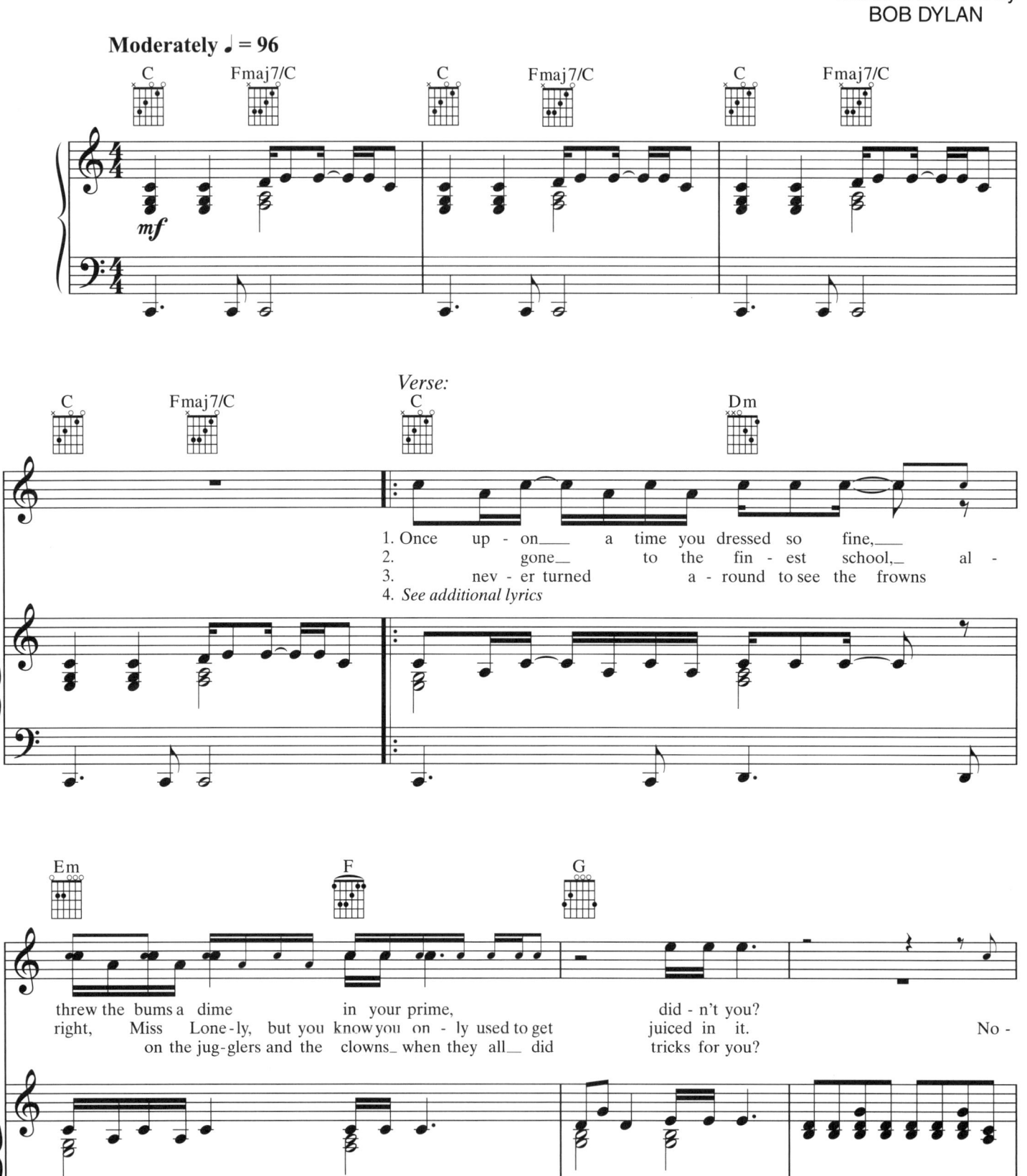

Moderately ♩ = 96

1. Once up-on___ a time you dressed so fine,___
2. ___ gone___ to the fin-est school,___ al-
3. ___ nev-er turned a - round to see the frowns
4. *See additional lyrics*

threw the bums a dime   in your prime,   did - n't you?
right, Miss Lone-ly, but you know you on - ly used to get   juiced in it.
on the jug-glers and the clowns___ when they all___ did   tricks for you?   No-

Like a Rolling Stone - 5 - 1

© 1965 (Renewed) SPECIAL RIDER MUSIC
Used by Permission of MUSIC SALES CORPORATION (ASCAP)
All Rights Reserved

Like a Rolling Stone - 5 - 2

F Em Dm C F Em
But now you don't__ talk so loud. Now you don't
he's not sell-ing an-y al-i-bis as you stare in-to the vac-uum
Ain't it hard when you dis-cov-er that he real-ly was-n't
Dm C Dm F
seem so proud a-bout hav-in' to be scroung-ing for your next
of his eyes and say, "Do you want to make a
where it's at af-ter__ he took from you ev-'ry-thing he could
Chorus:
G C F G
meal.
deal?"
steal?
1. How does it__ feel?__ How does it__ feel__
2.3.4. How does it__ feel?__ How does it__ feel__
C F G C F
to be with-out__ a home,__
to be on your__ own,__

like a com-plete un - known, like a roll-ing stone?
with no di - rec-tion home,

2. Oh, you've

a com-plete un-known, like a roll-ing stone?

3. Oh, you

Like a Rolling Stone - 5 - 4

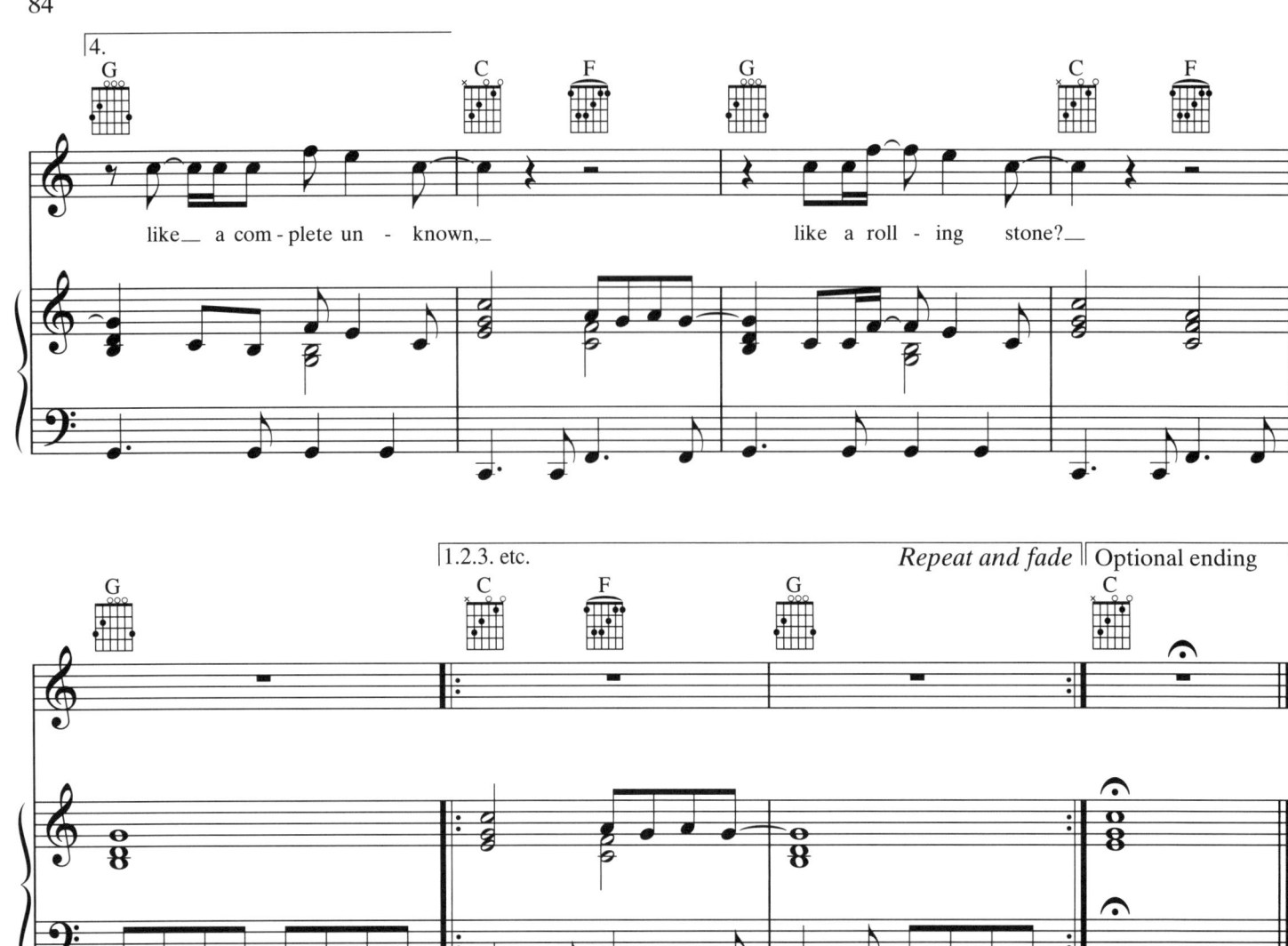

Verse 4:
Princess on the steeple and all the pretty people,
They're all drinkin', thinkin' that they got it made.
Exchanging all precious gifts,
But you better take your diamond ring,
You'd better pawn it, babe.
You used to be so amused
At Napolean in rags and the language that he used.
Go to him now, he calls you, you can't refuse.
When you got nothin', you got nothin' to lose.
You're invisible now, you got no secrets to conceal.
(*To Chorus:*)

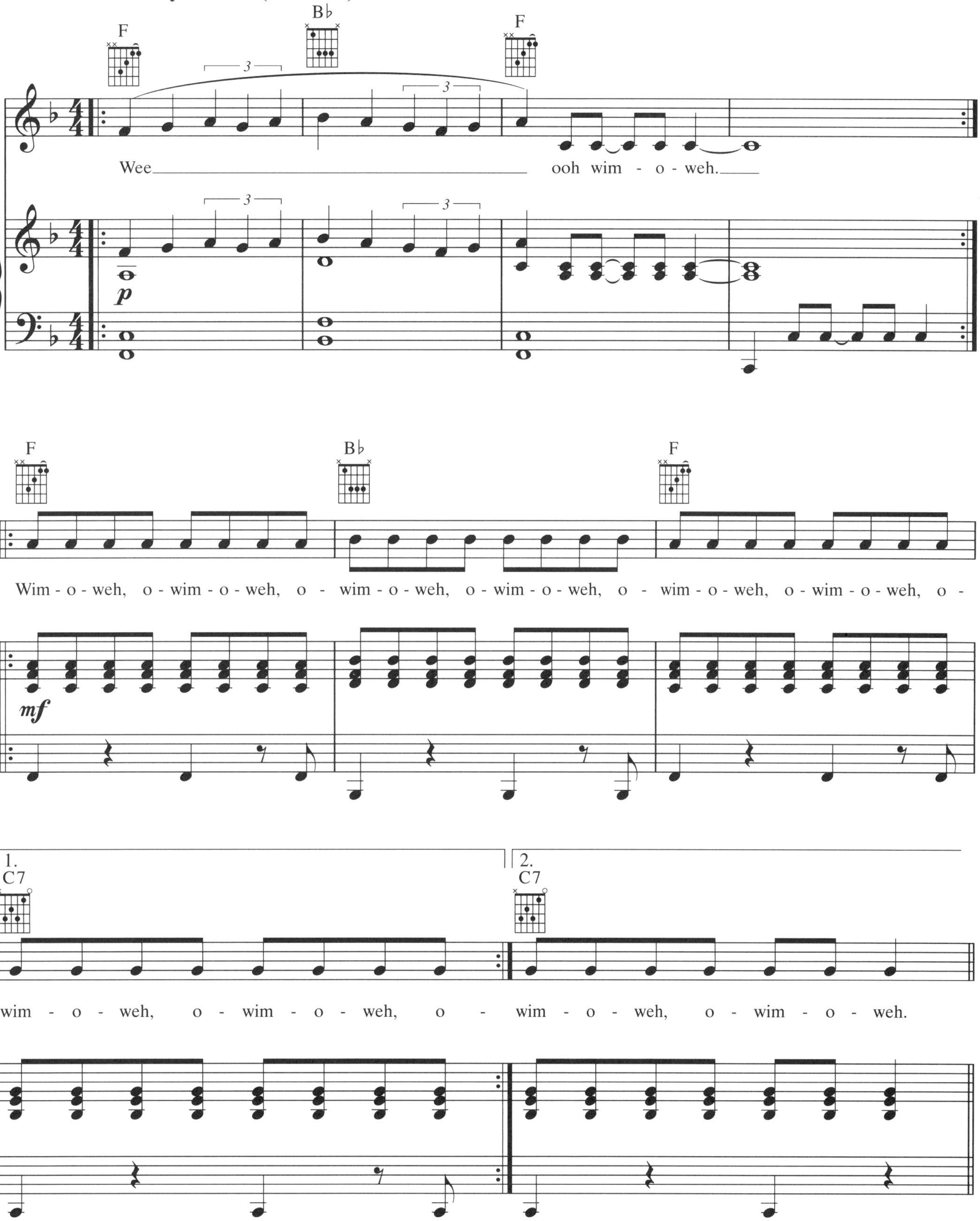

F
B♭
F
C7
1. In the jun - gle, the might - y jun - gle, the li - on sleeps to - night.
2. Near the vil - lage, the peace - ful vil - lage, the li - on sleeps to - night.
3. Hush, my dar - ling, don't fear, my dar - ling, the li - on sleeps to - night.
mp
F
B♭
F
C7
In the jun - gle, the might - y jun - gle, the li - on sleeps to - night.
Near the vil - lage, the peace - ful vil - lage, the li - on sleeps to - night.
Hush, my dar - ling, don't fear, my dar - ling, the li - on sleeps to - night.
mf
1.2.
F
B♭
F
C7
Wee ooh wim - o - weh.
Wim-o-weh, o-wim-o-weh, o - wim-o-weh, o-wim-o-weh, o - wim-o-weh, o-wim-o-weh, o - wim-o-weh, o-wim-o-weh.
(Bkgrd. vocals)

The Lion Sleeps Tonight - 3 - 3

MAMA TOLD ME NOT TO COME

Words and Music by
RANDY NEWMAN

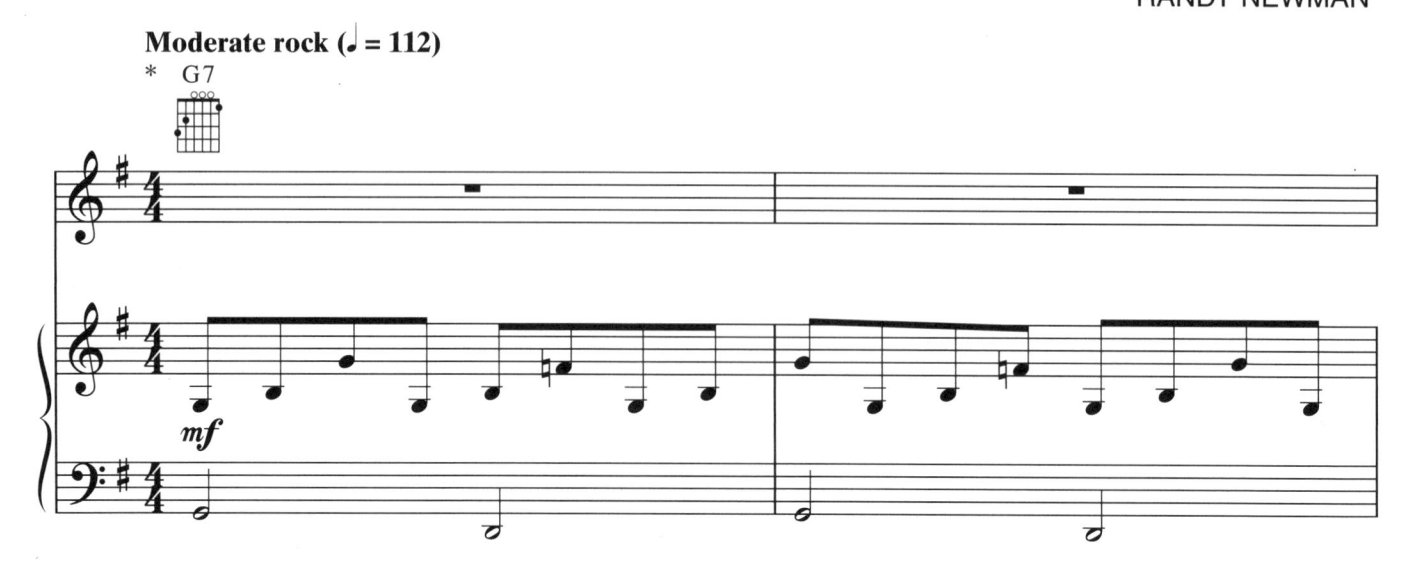

Moderate rock (♩ = 112)

(half sung, half spoken)

1. Want some

Verse:

whis-key in your wa-ter? Sug-ar in your tea?
2.3. See additional lyrics

* Original recording in A♭ Major

Mama Told Me Not to Come - 6 - 1

© 1966, 1970 (Copyrights Renewed) UNICHAPPELL MUSIC INC.
All Rights Reserved

What's all these cra - zy ques - tions they're ask - in' me?
This is the cra - zi - est par - ty that could ev - er be.
Don't turn on the lights 'cause I don't wan - na see. Ma - ma told
f
Chorus:
G
G7/B
C
E♭7/D♭
G
G7/B
C
me not to come.
Ma - ma told me not to come.

E♭7/D♭
G
1.
G7/B
C
E♭7/D♭
G
That ain't the way to have fun, no. Uh - uh.
(3rd time - She said,)
N.C.
2. 3.
G
G7/B
C
That ain't the way to have fun,
mf
E♭7/D♭
To Coda
G
N.C.
son.
That ain't the way to have fun, son.
G
G7/B
C
E♭7/D♭
G
G7/B
C
E♭7/D♭
G
(Guitar solo ad lib....

G7/B
C
E♭7/D♭
G
G7
D.S. 𝄋 al Coda
(after 3rd ending)
…end solo)
3. The
Coda
N.C.
That ain't the way to have fun,
no.
Shout Chorus:
G
G7/B
C
E♭7/D♭
G
Ma - ma told me, Ma - ma told me, Ma - ma told me, told me, told me.
(3 voices ad lib. freely)
G7/B
C
E♭7/D♭
G
G7/B
C
It's dan - ger - ous, oh yeah, yeah. Ma - ma told me not to go,

E♭7/D♭ G G7/B C E♭7/D♭ G
oh Ma - ma, Ma - ma. Ma - ma told me.
G G7/B C E♭7/D♭ G G7/B C
That ain't the way to have fun, no. That ain't the way to have fun,
E♭7/D♭ G G7/B C E♭7/D♭ G
son.
(more vocal ad libs.)
G7/B C E♭7/D♭ G G7/B C
That ain't the way to have fun, no. That ain't the way to have fun,

Verse 2:
(Spoken:)
Open up the window, let some air into this room.
I think I'm almost chokin' from the smell of stale perfume.
And that cigarette you're smokin' 'bout scare me half to death.
Open up the window, sucker, let me catch my breath.
(To Chorus:)

Verse 3:
(Spoken:)
The radio is blastin', someone's knockin' at the door.
I'm lookin' at my girlfriend; she's passed out on the floor.
I seen so many things I ain't never seen before.
Don't know what it is; I don't wanna see no more.
(To Chorus:)

(MEET) THE FLINTSTONES

Words and Music by
WILLIAM HANNA, JOSEPH BARBERA
and HOYT CURTIN

ly. ry.

Let's ride with the fam-'ly down the street,

through the cour-te-sy of Fred's two feet.

Half time
Fmaj7
Ab13
Gm7
C7(b9)
Fmaj7
you'll have a gay old time.
Swing
Gm7
Am7
We'll see Bar - ney, we'll ___ see Bet - ty, Bam - bam, Peb - bles,
Bbmaj7
Fmaj7
Ab13
Gm7
C7(b9)
Di - no, too. ___ You'll have a gay old
F6/9
E7(#9)
F6/9
E7(#9)
Fmaj7
time. ___

MONSTER MASH

Words and Music by
BOBBY PICKETT
and LEONARD CAPIZZI

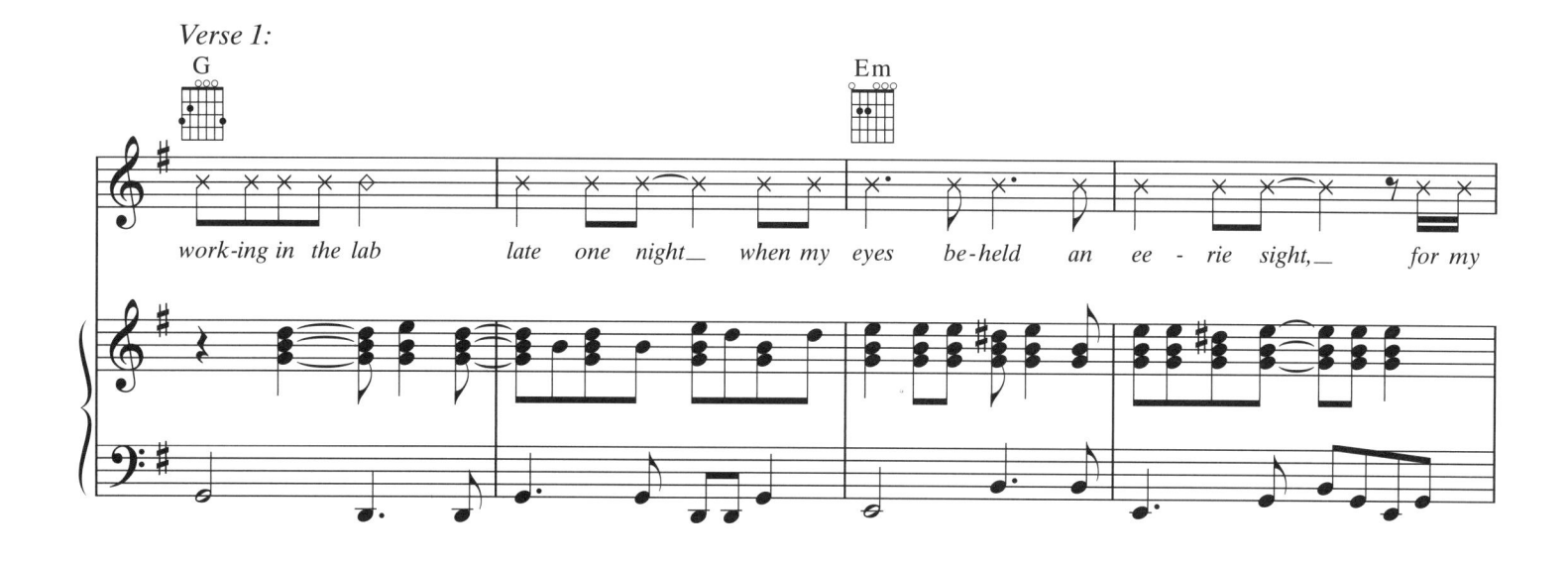

Moderately ♩ = 144

Verse 1:

1. I was working in the lab late one night when my eyes beheld an eerie sight, for my monster from his slab began to rise and suddenly, to my surprise...

(Bkgrd.) 1. He did the

Chorus 1:
G
Em
1. He did the Mon - ster Mash.
It was a
Mash,
the Mon-ster Mash.
C
grave-yard smash.
It caught on in a flash.
He did the Mash.
He did the
D
Verse 2:
G
He did the Mon - ster Mash.
2. From my lab - 'ra - to - ry in the
Mash.
Wha - ooh,
Em
cas - tle east to the mas - ter bed-room where the vam-pires feast, the
wha - ooh,
wha, wha -

Chorus 2:

Bridge:
C
D
zom-bies were_ hav-ing fun. The par-ty had just be-gun._ The
ooh, in a shoop, wha - ooh, in a shoop, wha -
C
D
N.C.
guests in - clud-ed Wolf - man, Drac - u - la, and his son. 3. The
ooh, in a shoop, wha - ooh. Wha -
Verses 3, 4, & 5:
G
Em
scene was rock-in', all were dig - gin' the sounds;_ I - gor on chains backed by
ooh,_ wha - ooh,_
4. 5. See additional lyrics
Am9
5
his bay - ing hounds. The cof - fin - bang - ers were a - bout to ar - rive__ with their
wha, wha - ooh,_ wha -

Choruses 3, 4, & 5:
D
G
vo-cal group, "The Crypt - Kick-er Five." 3. They played the Mon-
ooh. 3. They played the Mash,
4. 5. See additional lyrics
Em
ster Mash. the Mon-ster Mash. It was a grave-yard smash. They played the
C
D
Mash. It caught on in a flash. They played the Mash. They played the
1.2.
3.
Mon - ster Mash. Wha -
Mon - ster Mash. (Bkgrd.) Wha -

(Igor:) Mm, Mash good! (Boris:) Easy, Igor, you impetuous young boy. (Igor:) Mm, Mash good!

ooh, Mon-ster Mash, wha - ooh, Mon-ster Mash, wha -

Repeat ad lib. and fade

ooh, Mon-ster Mash, wha - ooh, Mon-ster Mash. Wha -

Verse 4:
Out from his coffin Drac's voice did ring.
Seems he was troubled by just one thing.
He opened the lid and shook his fist,
And said, "Whatever happened to my Transylvania Twist?"

Chorus 4:
(It's now the Mash,) It's now the Monster Mash,
(The Monster Mash.) and it's a graveyard smash.
(It's now the Mash.) It caught on in a flash.
(It's now the Mash.) It's now the Monster Mash.

Verse 5:
Now ev'rything's cool; Drac's a part of the band,
And my Monster Mash is the hit of the land.
For you, the living, this Mash was meant too.
When you get to my door, tell them Boris sent you.

Chorus 5:
(Then you can Mash,) Then you can Monster Mash,
(The Monster Mash.) and do my graveyard smash.
(Then you can Mash.) You'll catch on in a flash.
((Then you can Mash.) Then you can Monster Mash.

MUSTANG SALLY

Words and Music by
BONNY RICE

Moderate R&B ♩ = 116

Verse:

ly,
2. *See additional lyrics*

guess you bet-ter slow your Mus-tang down.

Mus-tang

Mustang Sally - 4 - 1

© 1968 (Renewed) FOURTEENTH HOUR MUSIC
All Rights Reserved

Lyrics:

Sal-ly, no, ba-by, guess you bet-ter slow your Mus-tang down.

You been run-nin' all o-ver town, now, oh, I guess I have to put your flat feet on the ground.

Mustang Sally - 4 - 2

Chorus:

All you wanna do is ride around, Sally. (Ride, Sally, ride.)

All you wanna do is ride around, Sally.

(Ride, Sally, ride.) All you wanna do is ride

around, Sally. (Ride, Sally, ride.) All you wanna do is a-ride

Verse 2:
I bought you a brand-new Mustang,
'Bout Nineteen sixty-five.
Now you come around, signifying a woman,
You don't wanna let me ride.
Mustang Sally, now, baby,
Guess you better slow that Mustang down.
You been runnin' all over town,
Oh, I've got to put your flat feet on the ground.
(To Chorus:)

Na Na Hey Hey Kiss Him Goodbye

Words and Music by
GARY DE CARLO, DALE FRASHUER and PAUL LEKA

With a beat

1. Na na na na na na na na, Hey hey hey, good-bye.
   na na na na na na, Hey hey hey, good-bye.

He'll ne-ver love you the way that I love you,
He's ne-ver near you to com-fort and cheer you,

'cause if he did no, no he would-n't make you cry.
When all those sad tears are falling baby from your eyes.

© 1969 (Renewed) UNICHAPPELL MUSIC, INC.
All Rights Reserved

Bb A7 Dm7 G7
He might be thrill - ing ba - by, but, my love's so dog - gone will - ing so
F Bb Bbm C6 F
kiss him, go on and kiss him good - bye. Na na
Ab 1 Eb F C7 2 Eb F C7
na na, Hey hey, hey, good - bye. Na na hey, hey good - bye. Na na
Repeat and Fade
F Ab Eb F C7
na na na na na na, Hey hey hey, good - bye. Na na

THE NIGHT THEY DROVE OLD DIXIE DOWN

Words and Music by
ROBBIE ROBERTSON

Moderately ♩ = 120

Verse:

1. Vir-gil Caine is my name, and I drove on the Dan-ville train,
2.3. *See additional lyrics*

'til so much cav-al-ry came and

*Recording in D flat major.

The Night They Drove Old Dixie Down - 4 - 1

© 1969 (Renewed) WB MUSIC CORP. and CANAAN MUSIC CORP.
All Rights Administered by WB MUSIC CORP.
All Rights Reserved

tore up the tracks a-gain. In the win-ter of 'Six-ty-five, we were hun-gry, just bare-ly a-live. I took the train to Rich-mond that fell; it was a time I re-mem-ber, oh, so well. The night

Chorus:

...they__ drove old Dix-ie down.__ And all the bells were ring-in' the night they__ drove old Dix-ie down.__ And all the peo-ple were sing-in'. They went: La la la la la la,__ la la la la la la la la__ la.

The Night They Drove Old Dixie Down - 4 - 3

Verse 2:
Back with my wife in Tennessee,
And one day she said to me,
"Virgil, quick come see.
There goes the Robert E. Lee."
Now, I don't mind I'm choppin' wood,
And I don't care if my money's no good.
Just take what you need and leave the rest,
But they should never have taken the very best.
(To Chorus:)

Verse 3:
Like my father before me,
I'm a working man.
And like my brother before me,
I took a rebel stand.
Well, he was just eighteen, proud and brave,
But a Yankee laid him in his grave.
I swear by the blood below my feet,
You can't raise the Caine back up
When it's in defeat.
(To Chorus:)

ONE

Words and Music by
HARRY NILSSON

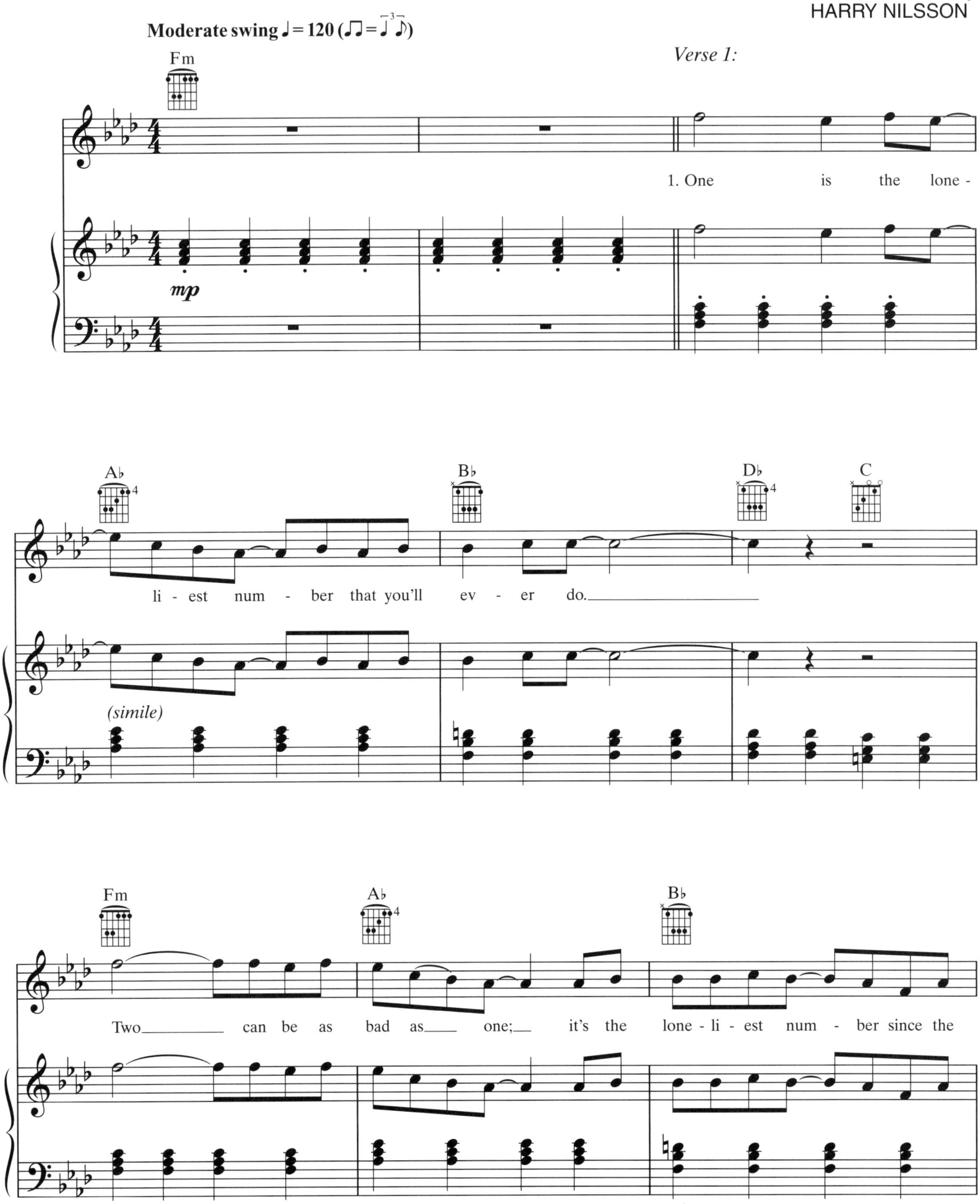

Verse 2:

number one._____

2. No is the sad - dest ex - pe - ri-ence you'll ev - er know._____ Yes, it's the sad - dest ex - pe - ri-ence you'll____ ev - er know.____ 'Cause

Chorus:

one is the lone-li-est num-ber that you'll ev-er do.___

___ One is the lone-li-est num-ber, whoa,___ worse than two.___

Bridge:

It's just no good an-y-more since you went a-way.___ Now I

Chorus:

spend my time just making rhymes of yesterday.

One is the loneliest number, one is the loneliest number, one is the loneliest number that you'll ever do.

Fm Ab Bb Db C
One is the lone - li-est, one___ is the lone - li-est, one_
Fm Ab Bb
___ is the lone - li - est num - ber that you'll ev - er do.___
Bridge:
Db C Fm7 Ab Amaj7 Fm7
It's just no good an - y - more_ since you went a - way.______
mp
Chorus:
N.C. Fm Ab
(Num - ber) One is the lone - li - est, (num - ber)
mf

B♭ D♭ C Fm
one is the lone - li - est, (num - ber) one is the lone-
A♭ B♭ 1.2. D♭ C
li - est num - ber that you'll ev - er do. (Num - ber)
3. D♭ C Fm A♭
(Num - ber) One is the lone - li - est num - ber that you'll
B♭ D♭ C N.C. A♭
ev - er do.

MACK THE KNIFE

English Words by
MARC BLITZSTEIN
Original German Words by
BERT BRECHT

Music by
KURT WEILL

Moderate swing ♩ = 84

1. Oh, the

Verses 1 & 2:

shark, babe, has such teeth, dear, and he shows them
shark bites with its teeth, babe, and scar-let bil-lows

pearl-y whites. Just a jack-knife
start to spread. Fan-cy gloves, though,

Mack the Knife - 7 - 1

© 1928 (Renewed) UNIVERSAL EDITION
© 1955 (Renewed) WEILL-BRECHT-HARMS CO., INC.
Renewal Rights Assigned to the KURT WEILL FOUNDATION FOR MUSIC, BERT BRECHT and THE ESTATE OF MARC BLITZSTEIN
All Rights Administered by WB MUSIC CORP.
All Rights Reserved

D♭dim7
Cm7
— has old — Mac-heath, — babe, — and he keeps it —
— has old — Mac-heath, — babe, — so there's nev - er, —
F7
B♭6
1.
2.
F♯7
out of sight. —
nev-er a trace — of red.
2. You know — when that
3. Now, on the
Verse 3:
B6
C♯m7
side-walk, uh-huh, huh, ooh, — Sun-day morn - ing, uh-huh, — lies a bod-
F♯7
B6
y — just ooz - ing life. And some-one's

B/D♯
Ddim7
C♯m7
sneak-ing 'round the cor - ner. Could that some-
F♯7sus
B6
G
one be Mack the Knife? 4. There's a
Verse 4:
C6
Dm7
tug-boat down by the riv - er, don't you know, where a ce -
G9
C6
ment bag's just a - droop - in' on down. Oh, that ce -

ment is just,___ it's there_ for the weight, dear.___ Five-'ll get you ten, Old___ Mack-ie's back in town.___ 5. Now, d'ja hear 'bout Lou-ie Mil-ler?___ He___ dis-ap-peared,_ babe,_ af-ter draw-ing out_ all_ his hard-earned cash. And now Mac-heath_ spends just like a sail-or. Could it be our boy's done some-thing rash? 6. Now, Jen-ny Div-

Verse 6:

er, yeah, Su-key Taw-dry, ooh, Miss Lot-te Len-ya, and old Lu-cy Brown. Ooh, the line forms on the right, babe, now that Mack-ie's back in town. 7. I said, Jen-ny Div-

Verse 7:
er, Su-key Taw-dry, look out to Miss Lot-te Len-ya, and old Lu-cy Brown. Yes, that

Eb/G F#dim7 N.C.
line forms on the right, babe, now that
Fm7 Bb7 Fm7 Bb7 Fm7 Bb7 N.C.
Mack - ie's back in
Eb Ab7 Eb Ab7
town.
Eb Ab7 Eb N.C. Eb9(#11)
Look out, old Mack-ie is back!

PEOPLE

Words by
BOB MERRILL

Music by
JULE STYNE

Moderately

pride hide all the need in-side, act-ing more like chil-dren than chil-dren. Lov-ers are ver-y spe-cial peo-ple; they're the luck-i-est peo-ple in the world. With one per-son, one ver-y spe-cial per-son, a feel-ing *deep in your soul* ____ *says, "You were half, now you're whole."* ____ *No more hunger and thirst, but first, be a person who needs people.* ____ *People who need people* ____ *are the luckiest people in the world.* ____ *world.* ____

PEOPLE GET READY

Words and Music by
CURTIS MAYFIELD

Moderately slow ♩ = 76

Don't need no tick-et,__ you just thank the Lord.
There's hope for all__ a-mong those loved the most.

Verse 3:

3. There ain't no room__ for the hope-less sin-ner who would hurt all man-kind__ just to save his own.__ Have pit-y on those__ whose chanc-es grow thin-ner, for there's

Lyrics:

no hiding place against the kingdom's throne. 4. So, people, get ready, there's a train a-comin'. You don't need no baggage, you just get on board. All you need is faith to hear the diesel hummin'. Don't need no ticket, you just thank the Lord.

PUFF (THE MAGIC DRAGON)

Words and Music by
PETER YARROW and LEONARD LIPTON

Verse:

1. Puff, the magic dragon, lived by the sea and
2.3.4. *See additional lyrics*

frol-icked in the au-tumn mist in a land called Hon-ah Lee.

© 1963 PEPAMAR MUSIC CORP.
Copyright Renewed and Assigned to SILVER DAWN MUSIC and HONALEE MELODIES
All Rights for SILVER DAWN MUSIC Administered by WB MUSIC CORP.
All Rights For HONALEE MELODIES Administered by CHERRY LANE MUSIC PUBLISHING COMPANY
All Rights Reserved

Puff (The Magic Dragon) - 3 - 1

A C♯m D A
Lit - tle Jack - ie Pa - per loved that ras - cal, Puff, and
D A F♯m B7 E7 A E7
bought him strings and seal - ing wax and oth - er fan - cy stuff. Oh!
Chorus:
A C♯m D A
Puff, the mag - ic drag - on, lived by the sea and
D A F♯m B7 E7
frol - icked in the au - tumn mist in a land called Hon - ah Lee.

Verse 2:
Together they would travel on a boat with billowed sail.
Jackie kept a lookout perched on Puff's gigantic tail.
Noble kings and princes would bow when'er they came.
Pirate ships would low'r their flag when Puff roared out his name. Oh!
(To Chorus:)

Verse 3:
A dragon lives forever, but not so little boys.
Painted wings and giant rings make way for other toys.
One grey night it happened; Jackie Paper came no more.
And Puff, that mighty dragon, he ceased his fearless roar. Oh!
(To Chorus:)

Verse 4:
His head was bent in sorrow; green scales fell like rain.
Puff no longer went to play along the cherry lane.
Without his lifelong friend, Puff could not be brave.
So Puff, that mighty dragon, sadly slipped into his cave. Oh!
(To Chorus:)

PIECE OF MY HEART

Words and Music by
JERRY RAGOVOY and BERT RUSSELL

Moderately slow ♩ = 80

Well, come on, come on, come on, come on.

Verse:

1. Did-n't I make you feel like you were the on - ly man?
2. *See additional lyrics*

Piece of My Heart - 6 - 2

Chorus:

take it! Take an-oth-er lit-tle piece of my heart___ now, ba-by. (Whoa,___

break it!) Break an-oth-er lit-tle bit of my heart.___ (Whoa,___

have a) Have an-oth-er lit-tle piece of my heart___ now, ba-by.___

Well, you know you got___ it, if it makes you feel good,___ oh, yes, in-deed.

2. You're makes you feel good.

Guitar solo ad lib.

I want you to

come___ on, come___ on, come___ on, come___ on and

Chorus:

[E] [A] [B] [A]

take it! Take an-oth-er lit-tle piece of my heart___ now, ba-by. (Whoa,___

[E] [A] [B] [A]

break it!) Break an-oth-er lit-tle bit of my heart.___ (Whoa,___

[E] [A] [B] [B♭]

have a) Have an-oth-er lit-tle piece of my heart___ now, ba-by.___

Verse 2:
You're out on the streets lookin' good,
And, baby, deep down in your heart
I guess you know that it ain't right.
Never, never, never, never, never,
Never hear me when I cry at night,
Baby, I cry all the time.
But each time I tell myself that I,
Well, I can't stand the pain.
But when you hold me in your arms,
I'll sing it once again.
I said come on, come on, come on, come on and…
(To Chorus:)

THE PINK PANTHER

By HENRY MANCINI

Moderately, mysterious ♩ = 120 (♫ = ♩♪ triplet)

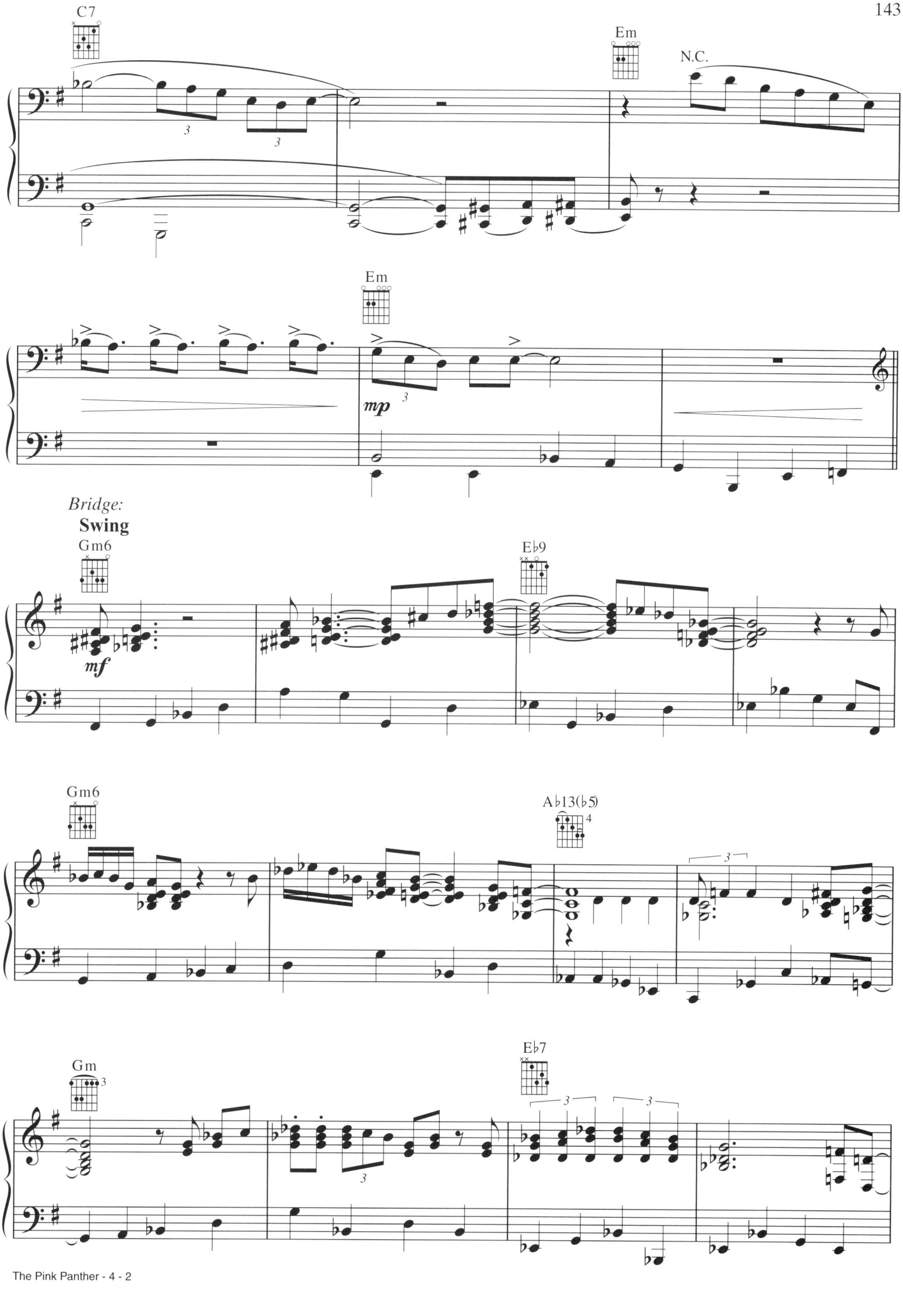
C7
Em
N.C.
Em
mp
Bridge:
Swing
Gm6
mf
E♭9
Gm6
A♭13(♭5)
Gm
E♭7

Gm
E♭9
D9
Gm6
3
3
Solo:
Em6
C13
Em6
(Inst. solo ad lib.…
F13
Em6
C13
Em6
C7
B7
Em
Tempo I
…end solo)
mp
mf

Verse:

RAINDROPS KEEP FALLIN' ON MY HEAD

Words by
HAL DAVID

Music by
BURT BACHARACH

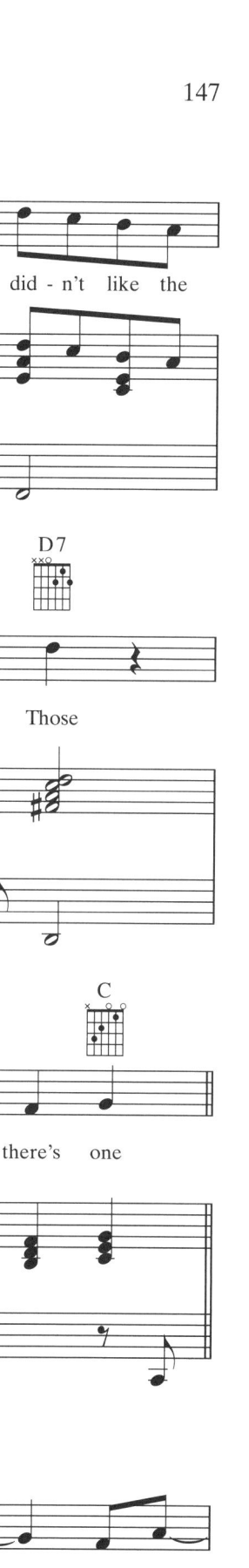

Verse 2:

did me some talkin' to the sun, and I said I didn't like the way he got things done, sleep-in' on the job. Those rain-drops are fall-in' on my head, they keep fall-in'. But there's one

Bridge:

thing I know: The blues they send to meet me. *Instrumental…*

148

me won't de-feat me. ...end Instrumental

It won't be long till hap-pi-ness steps up to greet me.

Verse 3:

3. Rain-drops keep fall-in' on my head, but that does-n't mean my eyes will soon be turn-in' red, cry-in's not for

Am7
D7
Gm7
me 'cause I'm nev - er gon - na stop the rain by com - plain - in',
B♭/C
C
F
Fmaj7
1.
Gm7
B♭/C
be - cause I'm free.
Noth - in's wor - ry - in'
2.
Gm7
B♭/C
N.C.
Noth - in's wor - ry - in' me.
Fast latin beat ♩ = 180
Repeat ad lib. and fade
Fmaj7
E♭maj7

SAVE THE LAST DANCE FOR ME

Words by
DOC POMUS

Music by
MORT SHUMAN

Moderately fast ♩ = 144

1. You can dance ev-'ry dance with the guy who gives you the eye; let him hold you tight.
You can
know that the mu-sic's fine, like sparkling wine. Go and have your fun. Laugh and
Go and car-ry on till the night is gone and it's time to go. If he

smile ev - 'ry smile for the man who held
sing, but while we're a - part don't give
asks if you're all a - lone, can he
E
your hand 'neath the pale moon - light. But
your heart to an - y - one. But
take you home, you must tell him no. 'Cause
don't for -
Chorus:
A
E
get who's tak - ing you home and in whose arms you're gon - na be.
B7
So, dar - lin', save the last dance for

Bridge:

me. Mm.___ 2. Oh, I ___ Ba-by, don't you know I

love you so?___ Can't you feel it when we touch?

I will nev-er, nev-er let you go.___ I love you, oh, so

much. 3. You can

Coda
E7
A
'Cause don't for - get who's tak - ing you home__ and in__ whose arms you're
E
B7
gon - na be. So, dar - lin', save the
E
last dance__ for__ me. Mm.__
B7
E
Repeat ad lib. and fade
Save the last dance_ for__ me. Mm.__

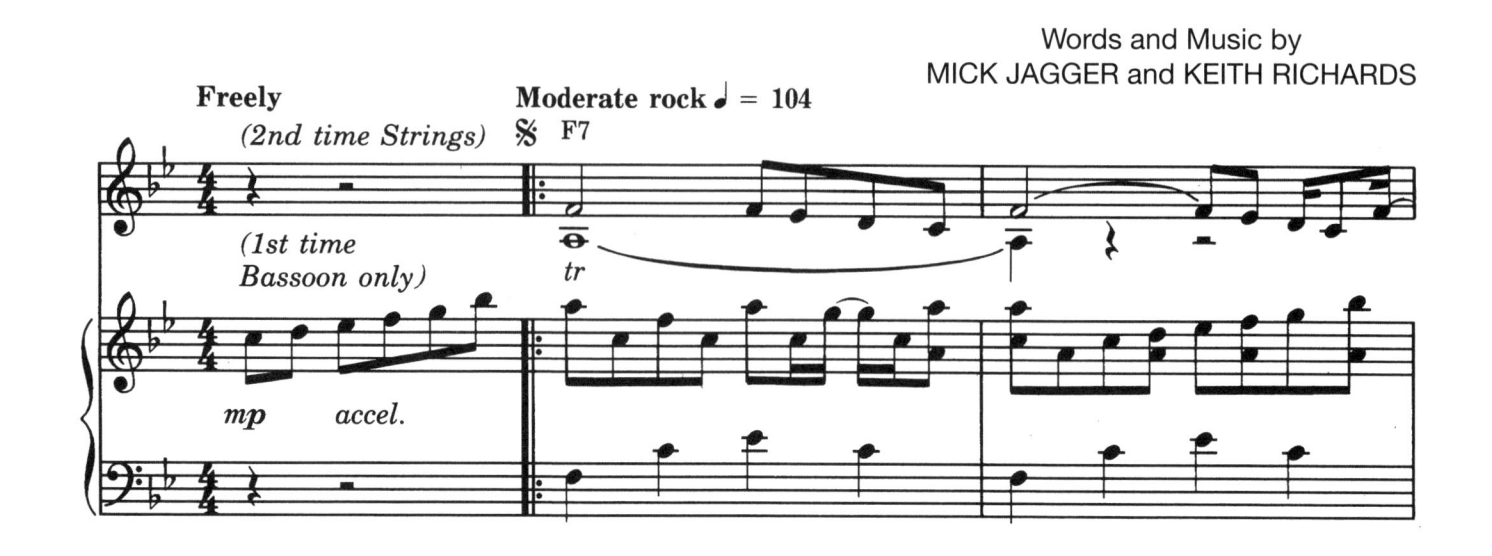

SHE'S A RAINBOW

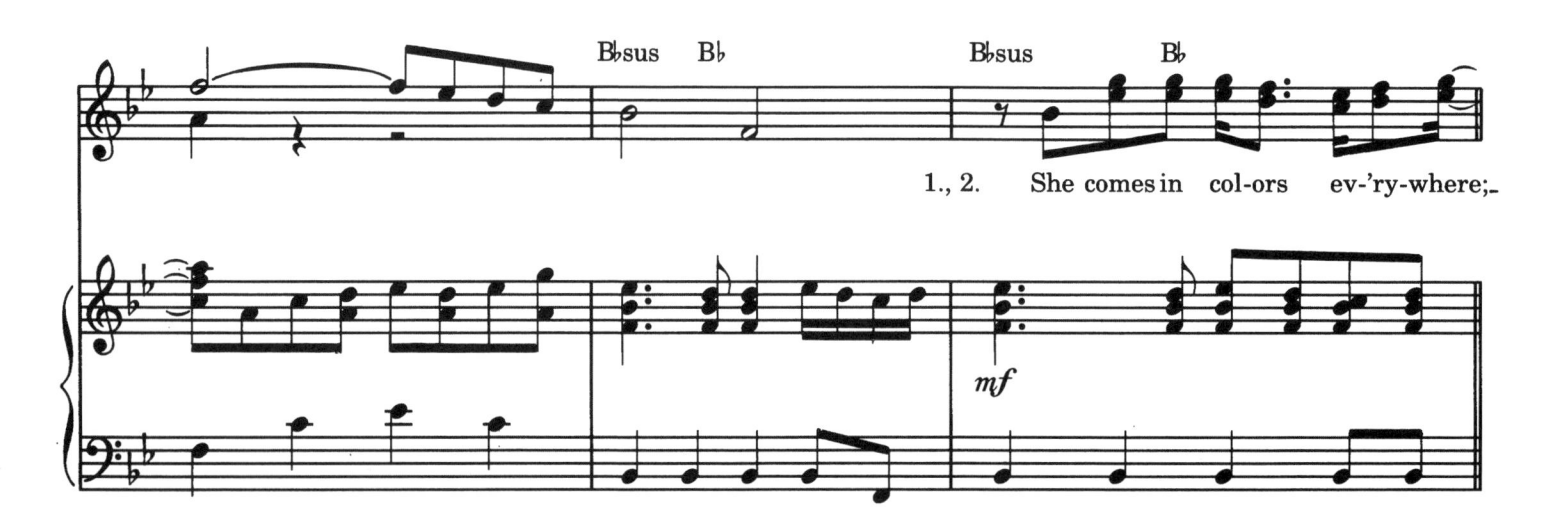

Words and Music by
MICK JAGGER and KEITH RICHARDS

Chorus:
E♭
B♭sus B♭
B♭sus B♭
she combs her hair. She's like a rain - bow,
B♭sus B♭
E♭
B♭
com-ing, col-ors in the air. Oh, ev'ry - where, she comes in
F7
B♭
To Coda
col - ors. Wanh, wanh, la-la - la.
freely

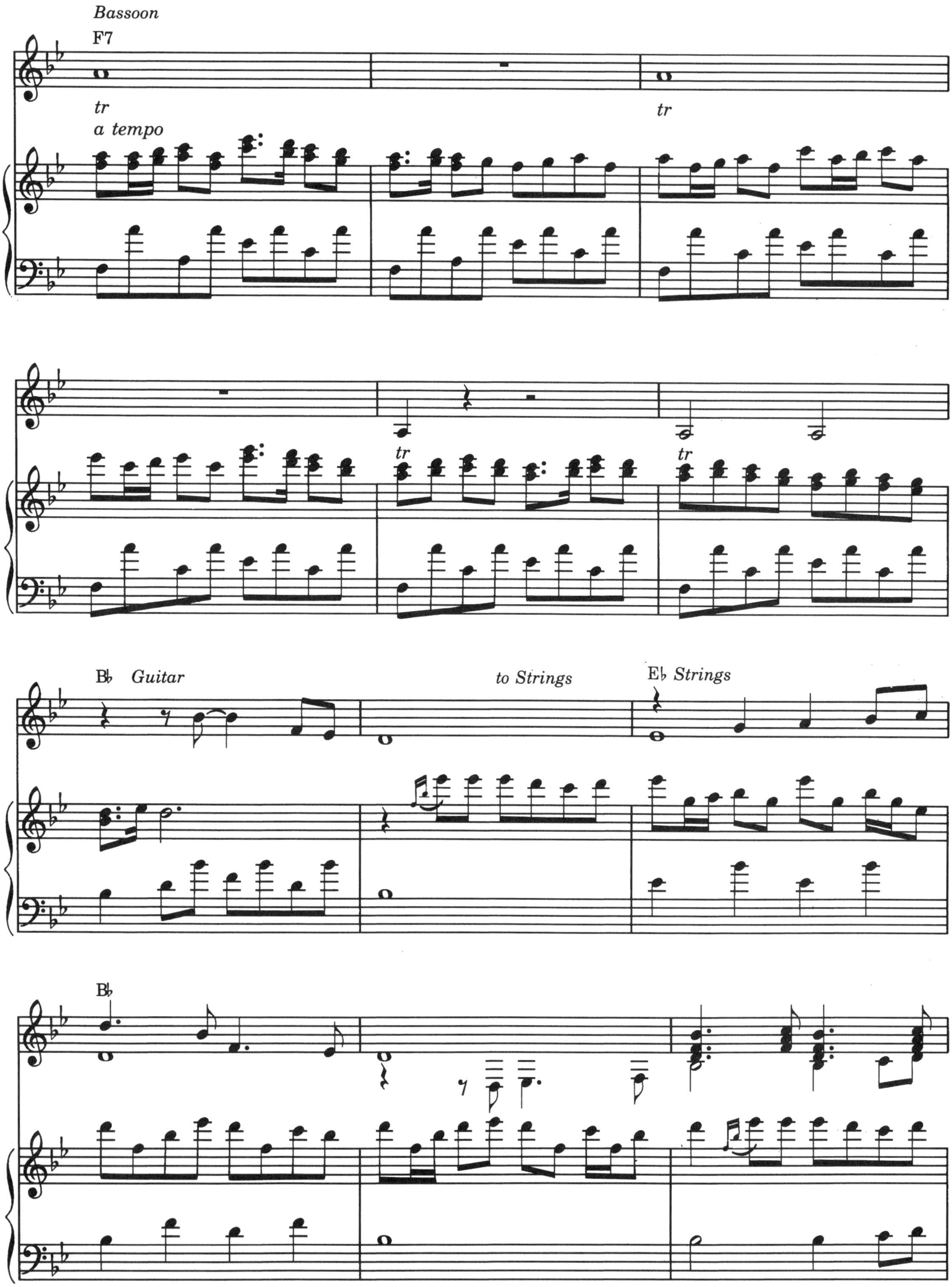
Bassoon
F7
tr
a tempo
tr
tr
tr
B♭ Guitar
to Strings
E♭ Strings
B♭

E♭
B♭
F7
B♭
Freely
Verse
8va
1. Have you seen her dressed in
F
a tempo
blue?
(2.) gold?
See the sky_ in front of
Like a queen_in days of
you;
old,

F
and her face is like a sail, speck of white so fair and pale.
She shoots her col-ors all a-round like a sun-set go-ing down.
Have you seen a la-dy
B♭sus B♭
fair-er?
B♭sus B♭
She comes in col-ors ev-'ry-where;
Chorus
E♭sus E♭
she combs her
B♭sus B♭
hair.
She's like a
B♭sus B♭
rain-bow,
B♭sus B♭
com-ing, col-ors in the

She's a Rainbow - 6 - 6

SOUL MAN

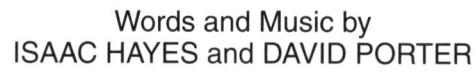

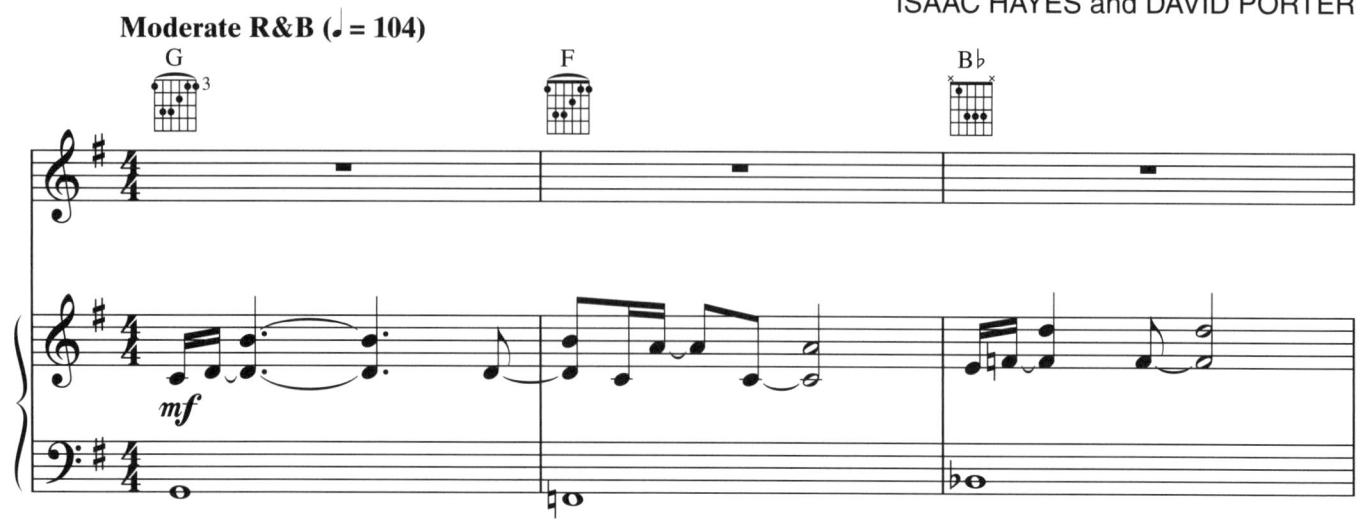

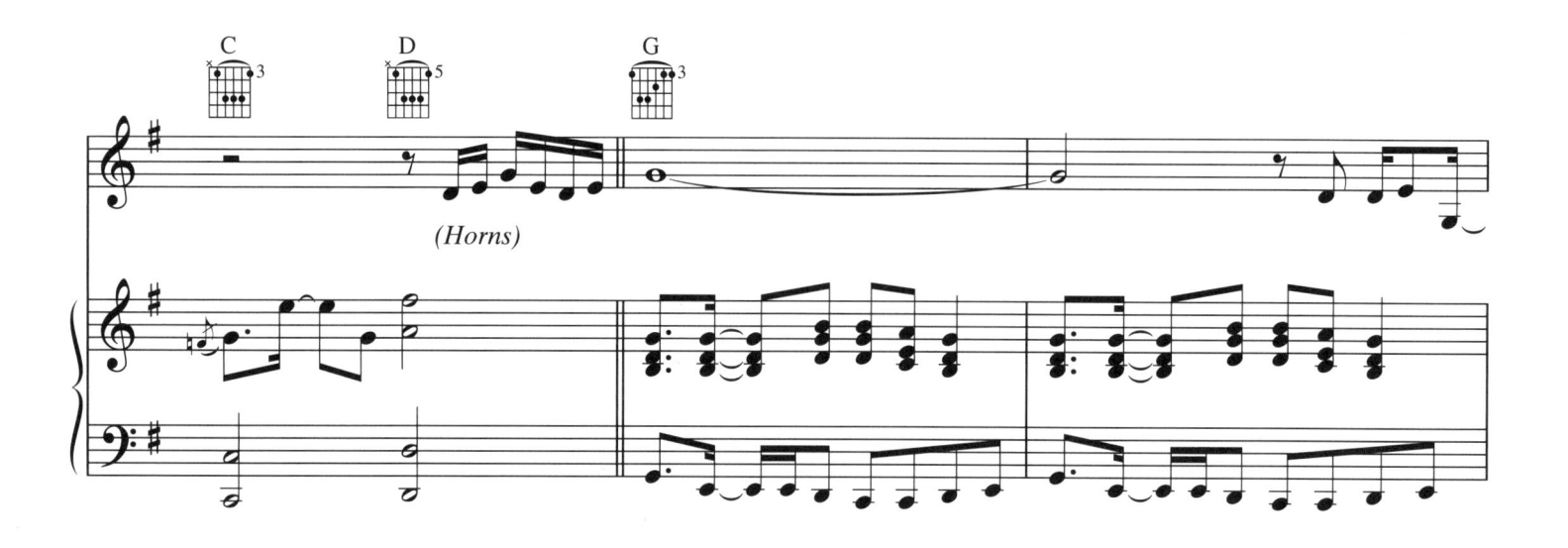

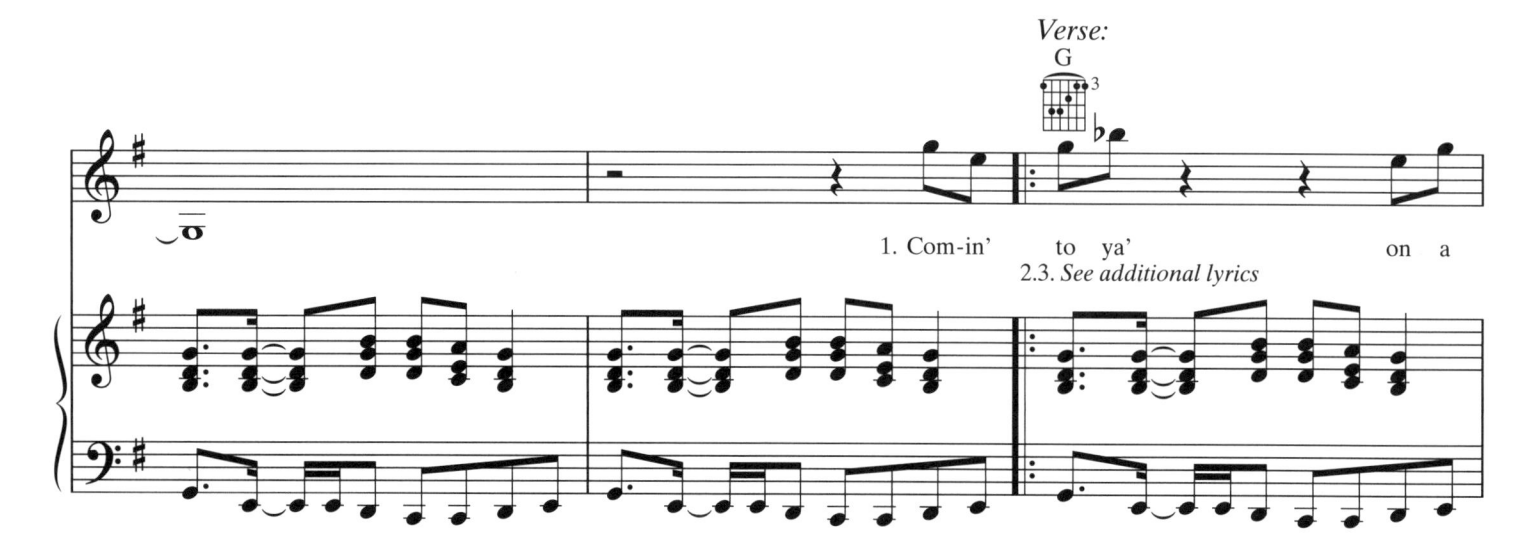

Words and Music by
ISAAC HAYES and DAVID PORTER

Moderate R&B (♩ = 104)

dust - y road;
good lov - in', I got a truck - load. And
when you get it, you got some. So, don't wor - ry, 'cause
Chorus:
G
3
F
I'm com - in'. I'm a soul man, I'm a
G
3
soul man. I'm a soul man,

F
G
1.2.
C
D
I'm a soul man.
2. Got
3. I was
3.
C
D
Bridge:
E♭
B♭
Grab the rope and I'll pull you in,
C
C/D
D♭/E♭
give you hope, and be your on - ly boy - friend, yeah, yeah, yeah, yeah.
A♭
G♭
B

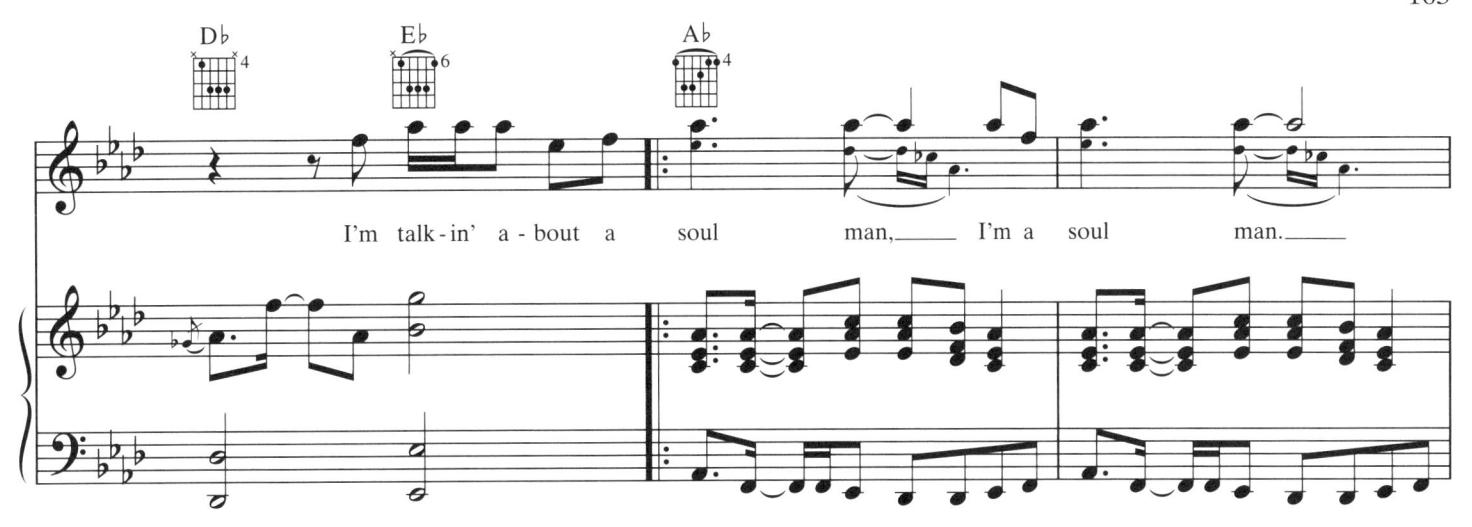

Verse 2:
Got what I got the hard way,
And I'll make it better each and every day.
So, honey, don't you fret,
'Cause you ain't seen nothin' yet.
(To Chorus:)

Verse 3:
I was brought up on a side street.
Listen now, I learned how to love before
I could eat.
I was educated at Woodstock.
When I start lovin', oh, I can't stop.
(To Chorus:)

The Sound of Silence

Words and Music by
PAUL SIMON

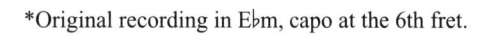

Moderately ♩ = 104

Verse 1:

1. Hello, darkness, my old friend, I've come with talk to you again. Because a vision softly creeping left its seeds while I was sleeping.

*Original recording in E♭m, capo at the 6th fret.

© 1964 (Renewed) PAUL SIMON
Used by Permission of MUSIC SALES CORPORATION (ASCAP)
All Rights Reserved

F C Am
C G Em
And the vi - sion that was plant-ed in my brain still re - mains
C G A2
G D E2
with-in the sound of si - lence.
2. In rest - less dreams I walked a -
Verse 2:
G Am
D Em
lone, nar - row streets of cob-ble - stone. 'Neath the ha - lo of a
F C F C
C G C G
street - lamp I turned my col - lar to the cold and damp,

166

Lyrics:

when my eyes were stabbed by the flash of a ne-on light that split the night and touched the sound of si-lence.

Verse 3:
3. And in the na-ked light I saw ten thou-sand peo-ple, may-be more. Peo-ple talk-ing with-out speak-ing, peo-ple hear-ing with-out lis-t'ning.

F
C
C
G
Peo-ple writ-ing songs that voic-es nev-er share__ and no one
Am
C
G
Am
Em
G
D
Em
dared dis-turb the sound of si-lence.
Verse 4:
G
Am
D
Em
4. "Fools," said I, "you do not know, si-lence like a can-cer grows.
F
C
F
C
C
G
C
G
Hear my words that I might__ teach you,__ take my arms that I might__ reach you."__

F
C
C
G
But my words like si - lent rain - drops fell
Am
Em
C
G
G
D
and ech - oed in the wells of
Am
Em
Verse 5:
G
D
si - lence. 5. And the peo - ple bowed and prayed
Am
Em
to the ne - on god they made. And the sign flashed out its

F C F C
C G C G
warn - ing in the words that it was form - ing.
F
C
And the sign said, "The words of the proph - ets are writ - ten on the sub - way walls
C Am C
G Em G
and ten - e - ment halls" and whis - pered in the
G A2 Am
D E2 Em
sounds of si - lence.
rit.

THEME FROM "A SUMMER PLACE"

Music by
MAX STEINER

Slowly, in 2 ♩. = 63

Theme From "A Summer Place" - 4 - 1

© 1960 (Renewed) WB MUSIC CORP.
All Rights Reserved

Theme From "A Summer Place" - 4 - 2

F Dm7 Gm7 C9 F Dm7 Gm7 C9
F Dm7 Gm7 C9 F Dm7
Gm7 C9 F
cresc.
D Bm7 Em7 A9 D Bm7 Em7 A9
mf
D Bm7 Em7 A9 D Bm7 Em7 A9

Repeat ad lib. and fade

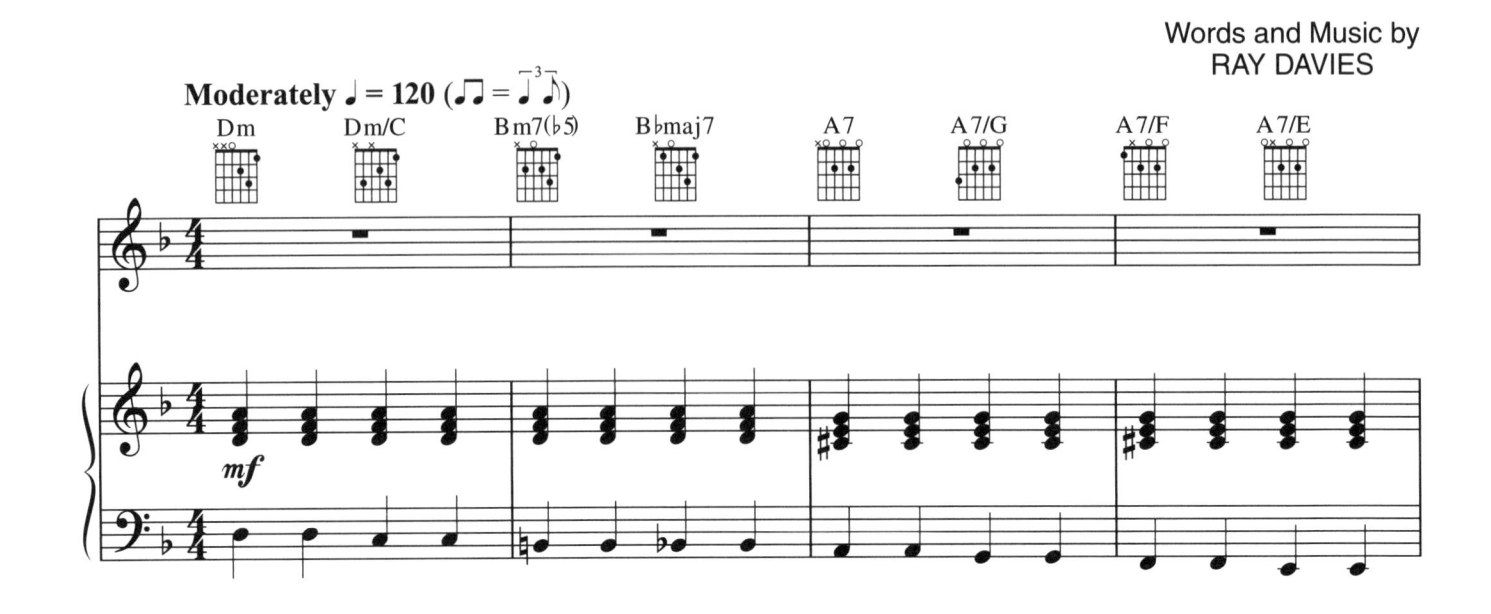

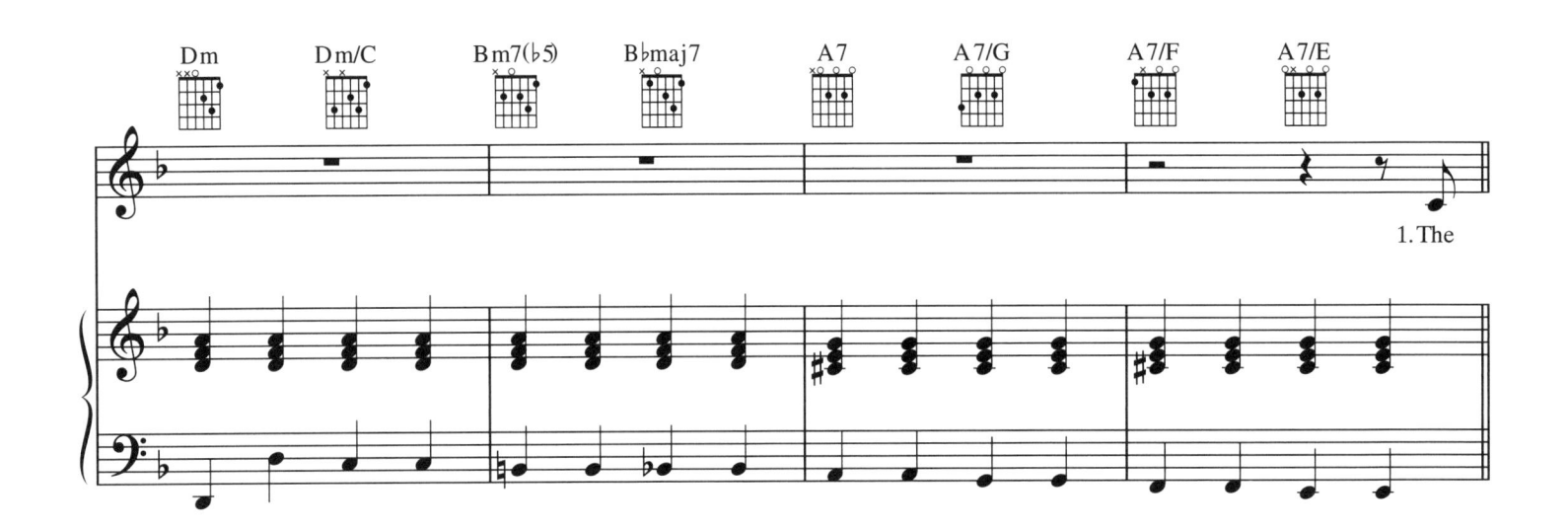

SUNNY AFTERNOON

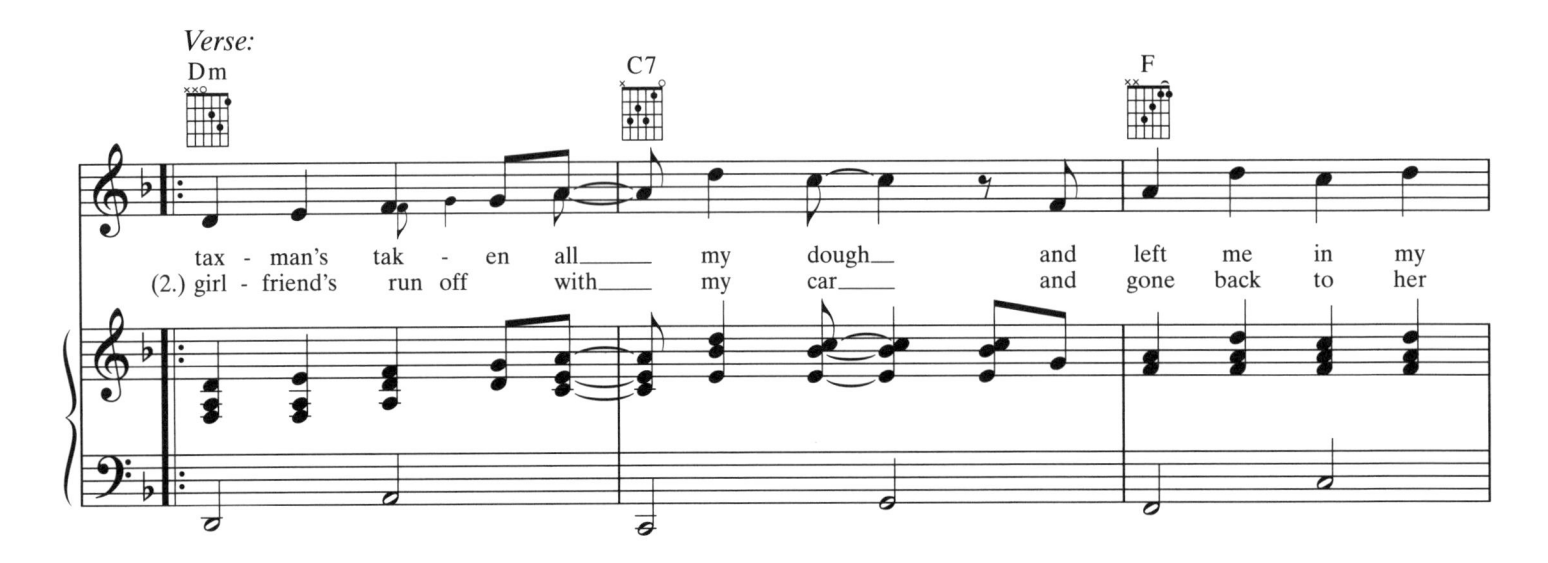

Words and Music by
RAY DAVIES

Moderately ♩ = 120

Verse:

The tax-man's taken all my dough and left me in my
(2.) girl-friend's run off with my car and gone back to her

C7 A7 A7/G A7/F A7/E
state - ly home, laz - ing on a sun - ny af - ter - noon.
ma and pa, tell-ing tales of drunk - en - ness and cruel -
Dm C7 F C7
And I can't sail my yacht; he's tak - en ev - 'ry - thing I've got.
ty. Now I'm sit - tin' here, sip - pin' at my ice - cold beer,
A7 A7/G A7/F A7/E Dm
All I've got's this sun - ny af - ter - noon.
laz - ing on a sun - ny af - ter - noon.
D7 G7
1. 3. Save me, save me, save me from this squeeze.
2. Help me, help me, help me sail a - way.

C7
I got a big fat mom - ma try'n' to break
You give me two good rea - sons why I ought to
F
A7
Dm
me.
stay.
And I love to live so
'Cause I love to live so
G9
Dm
G7
C7
pleas - ant - ly,
pleas - ant - ly,
live this life of lux - u - ry,
live this life of lux - u - ry,
F
A7
Dm
Dm/C
Bm7(♭5)
B♭maj7
laz - ing on a sun - ny af - ter - noon, in - a
laz - ing on a sun - ny af - ter - noon, in - a

Dm/A Dm/G A7/F A7/E Dm Dm/C Bm7(♭5) B♭maj7
sum-mer - time, in - a sum-mer - time, in - a
sum-mer - time, in - a sum-mer - time, in - a
Dm/A Dm/G 1. A7/F A7/E 2. A7/F A7/E D.S. 𝄋
sum - mer - time. 2. My Ah,
sum - mer - time.
3. A7/F A7/E Dm Dm/C Bm7(♭5) B♭maj7
in - a sum - mer - time, in - a
Dm/A Dm/G A7/F A7/E
N.C.
Repeat and fade
sum - mer - time.

SUNSHINE OF YOUR LOVE

Words and Music by
JACK BRUCE, PETE BROWN
and ERIC CLAPTON

Moderately ♩ = 102

1. It's get-ting near dawn,
(2. 4.) with you, my love,
3. (Inst. solo ad lib....

when lights close their tir-ed eyes. I'll
the light's shin-ing through on you. Yes, I'm

soon be with you,___ my___ love,___ to give you my dawn___ sur-prise.___
with you, my love,___ it's the morn-ing and just___ we___ two.___

___ I'll be with you, dar-ling, soon,___ I'll
I'll stay with you, dar-ling, now,___ I'll

be with you when___ the stars___ start___ fall-ing.
stay with you till___ my seas___ are___ dried___ up.

To Coda ⊕

Chorus:
A C G A C G
I've been wait - ing so long to be where I'm go - ing
A C G A
in the sun - shine of your love.
1.
D C D N.C.
2. 3.
2. I'm
...end solo)
D C D N.C. D C D N.C.
D.S. 𝄋 al Coda
4. I'm

Coda

I've been waiting so long, I've been waiting so long.

I've been waiting so long to be where I'm going

in the sunshine of your love.

Repeat and fade

SWEET SOUL MUSIC

Words and Music by
SAM COOKE,
with Additional Material by
ARTHUR CONLEY and OTIS REDDING

Verse 1:

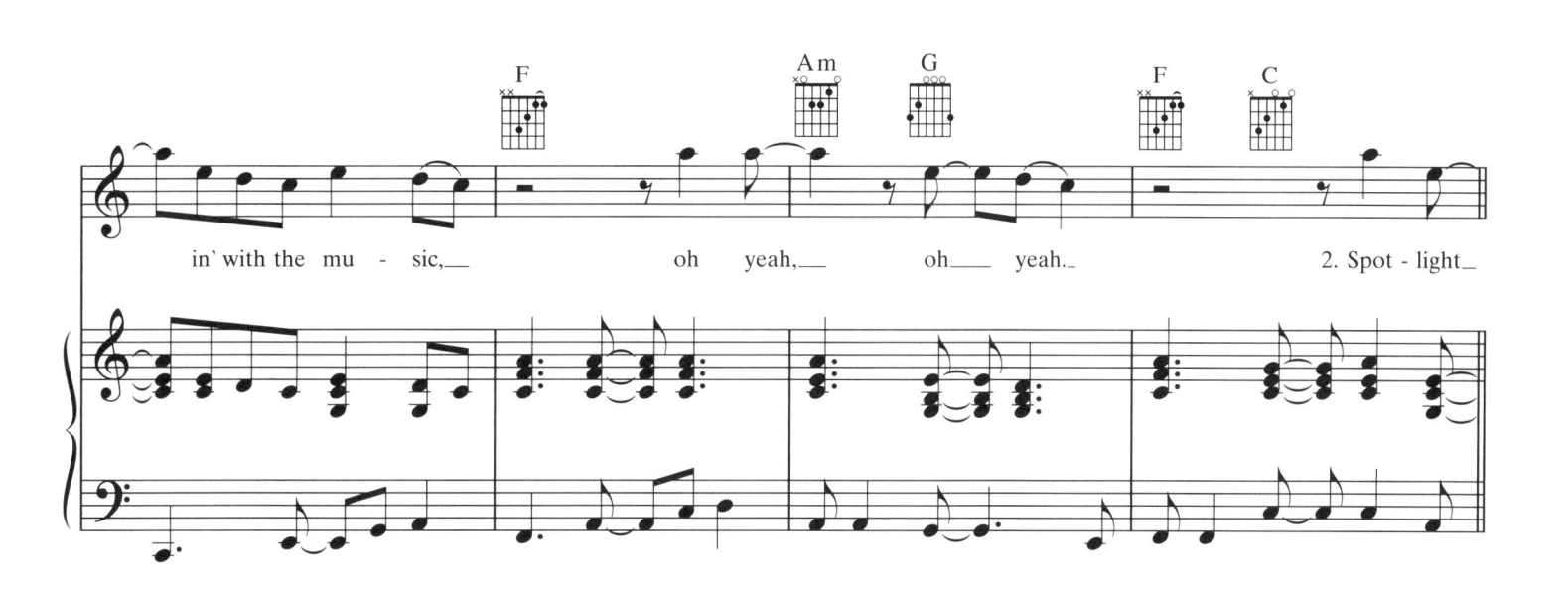

(Bkgrd. vocals cont. sim. to end)

___ on the floor, ya'll, ___ a - go - in' to a go - go, danc - in' with the mu - sic, ___ oh yeah, ___ oh ___ yeah. ___ 2. Spot - light ___

Verses 2, 3, & 4:

___ on Lou Rawls, ya'll. ___ Oh, don't ___ he look boss, ya'll, ___
___ on Sam and Dave, ya'll. Oh, don't ___ they look great, ya'll, ___
___ on Wil - son Pick - ett, now, that wick - ed, wick - ed Pick - ett, ___

sing - in' "Love's__ A Hurt - in' Thing," ya'll,__ oh yeah,__
sing - in' "Hold__ On, I'm Com - in',"__ oh yeah,__
sing - in' "Mus - tang Sal - ly,"__ oh yeah,__

__ oh,__ oh yeah.__ 3. Spot - light__ 5. Spot - light__
__ oh,__ oh yeah.__ 4. Spot - light__
__ oh,__ oh yeah.__

Verse 5:

__ on O - tis Red - ding, now, sing - in' "Fa__ fa fa fa fa fa fa,__

__ ha, fa fa__ fa fa fa fa fa fa."__ Oh yeah,__

Sweet Soul Music - 5 - 3

Am G F C
oh, oh yeah. Get it, O - tis.
F C F C F C N.C.
6. Spot - light
Verse 6:
F C
on James Brown, ya'll. He's the king of them all, ya'll. He's the king
F Am G F C
of them all, ya'll, oh yeah, oh, oh yeah. Do you like

Chorus:

[F] __ good mu-sic? __ That sweet __ soul mu - sic? [C] Just long __

[F] __ as it's swing - in', __ [Am] oh yeah, __ [G] oh, __ oh yeah. __ [F] [C] I got __

__ to get the feel - in'. I got __ to get the feel - in'. Do you like __

Repeat ad lib. and fade

__ good mu - sic? __ That sweet __ soul mu - sic? Do you like __

Verse 2:
I picked up my bag, I went lookin' for a place to hide,
When I saw Carmen and the devil walkin' side by side.
I said, "Hey, Carmen, come on, let's go downtown."
He said, "I gotta go, but my friend can stick around."
(To Chorus:)

Verse 3:
Go down, Miss Moses, there's nothing that you can say.
It's just old Luke and Luke's waitin' on the Judgment Day.
I said, "Luke, my friend, what about young Anna Lee?"
He said, "Do me a favor, son, won't you stay and keep Anna Lee company."
(To Chorus:)

Verse 4:
Crazy Chester followed me and he caught me in the fog.
He said, "I'll fix your rack if you'll take Jack, my dog."
I said, "Wait a minute, Chester, you know I'm a peaceful man."
He said, "That's okay, boy, won't you feed him when you can."
(To Chorus:)

Verse 5:
Catch a cannonball, now, take me down the line.
My bag is sinkin' low and I do believe it's time
To get back to Miss Fanny, you know she's the only one
Who sent me here with her regards for everyone.
(To Chorus:)

TAKE FIVE

By PAUL DESMOND

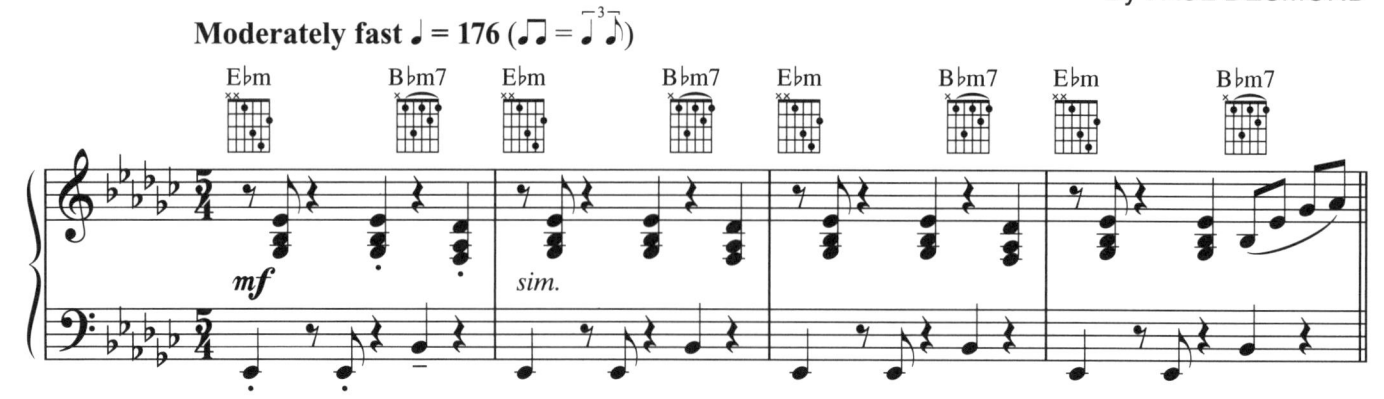

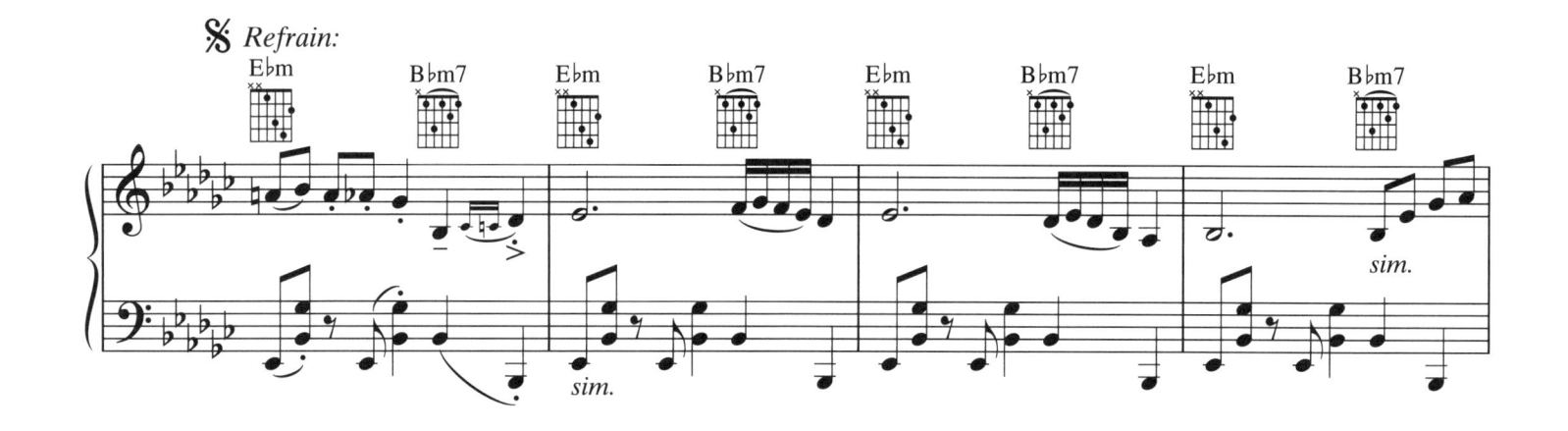

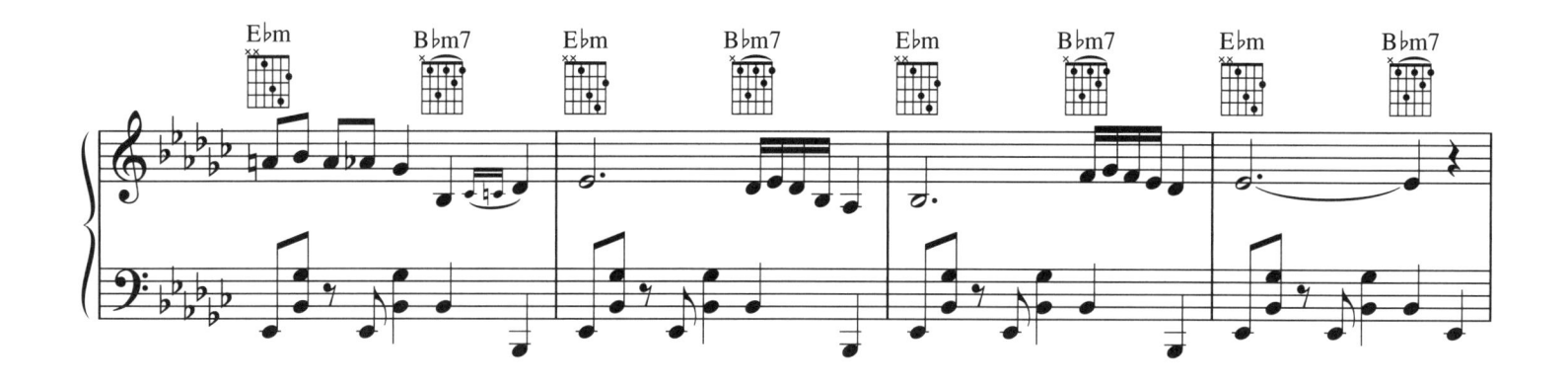

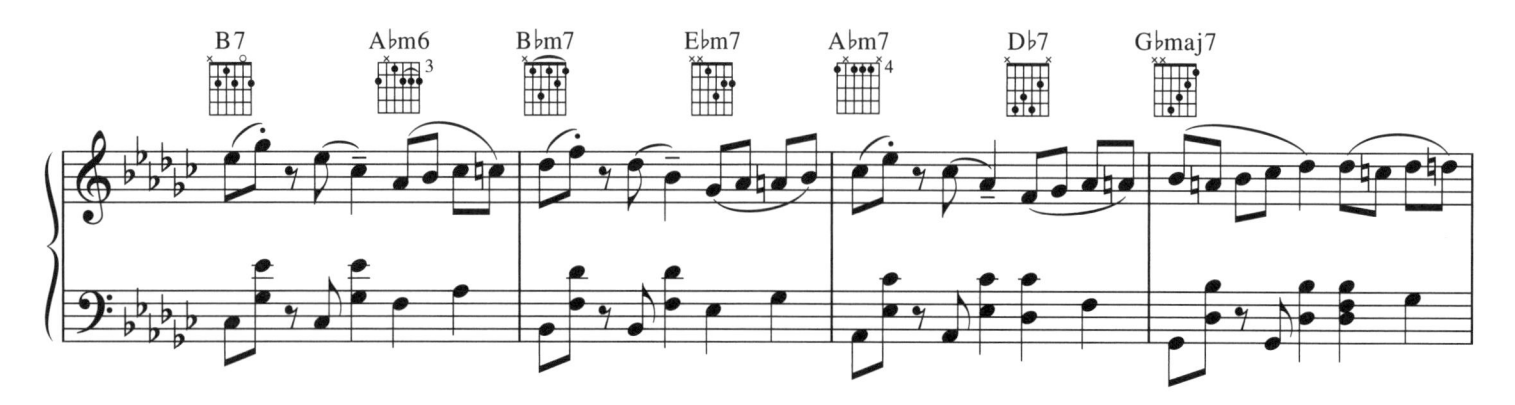

Moderately fast ♩ = 176

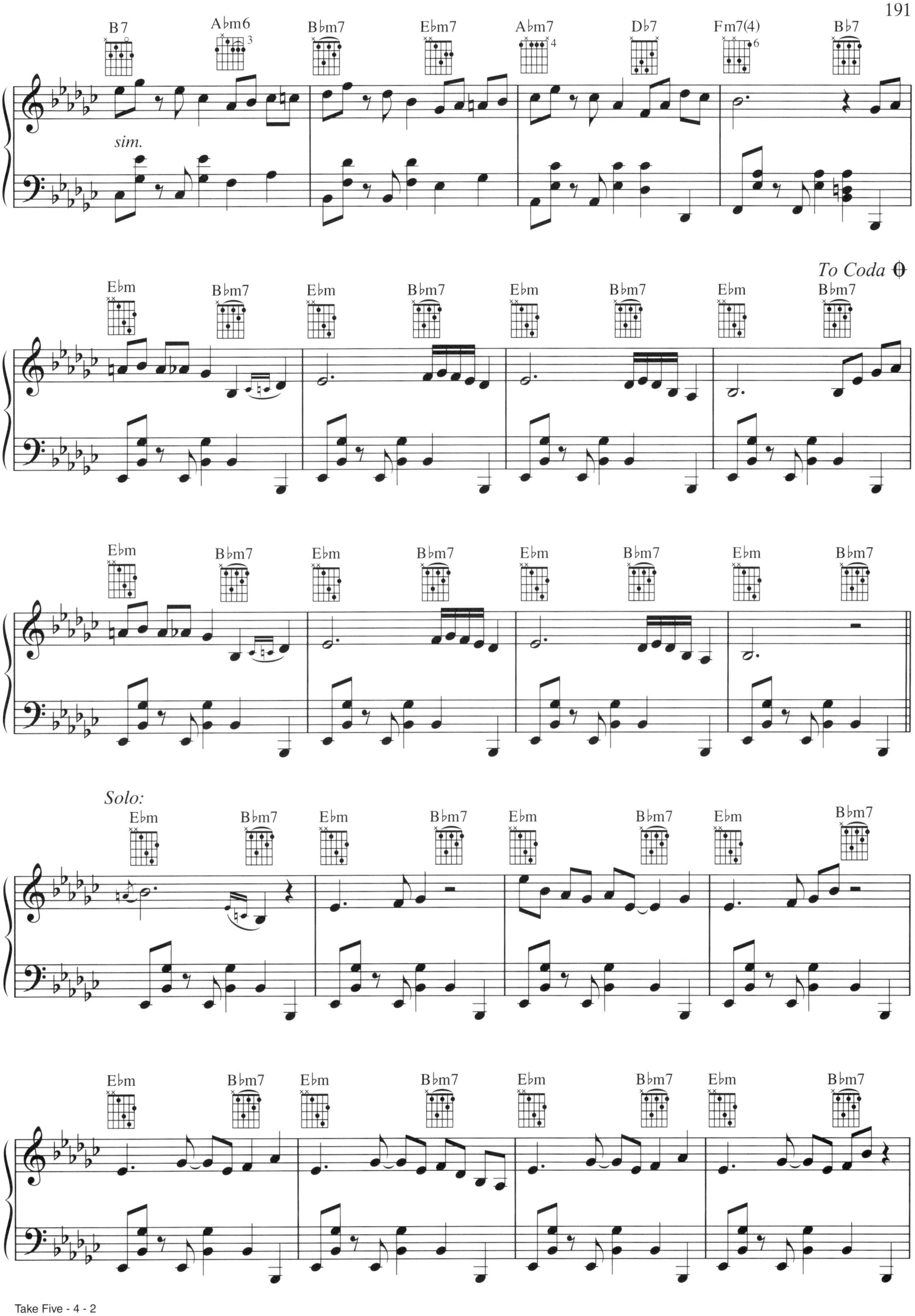
B7
A♭m6
B♭m7
E♭m7
A♭m7
D♭7
Fm7(4)
B♭7
sim.
To Coda
E♭m
B♭m7
Solo:

192

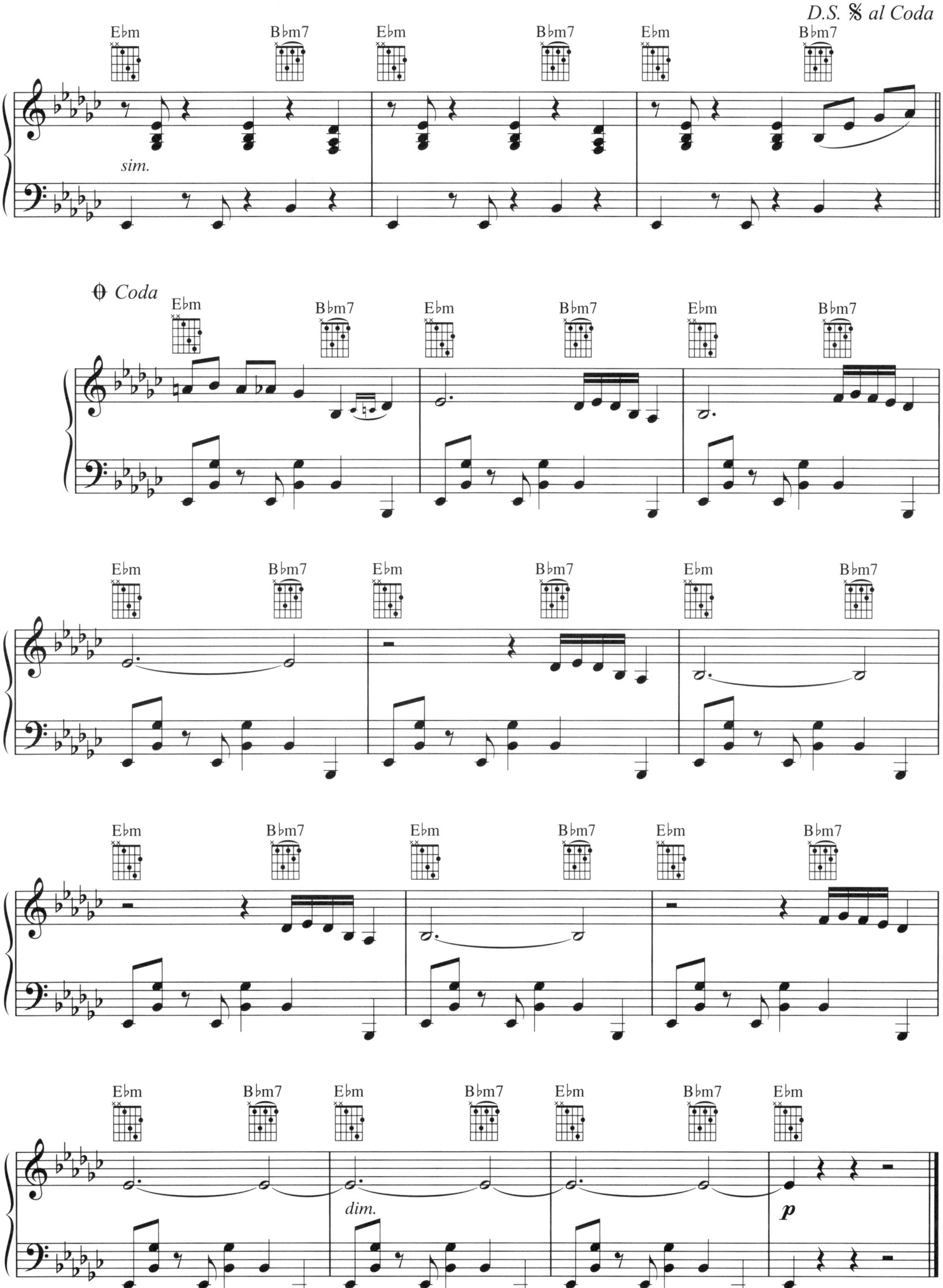
D.S. 𝄋 al Coda
Ebm
Bbm7
sim.
𝄌 Coda
dim.
p

(What a) Wonderful World

Words and Music by
SAM COOKE, HERB ALPERT
and LOU ADLER

Moderately ♩ = 120

Verse:

1.3. Don't know much a-bout his-to-ry.___ Don't know much bi-
2. Don't know much a-bout ge-og-ra-phy.___ Don't know much trig-o-

ol-o-gy.___ Don't know much a-bout a sci-ence book.___
nom-e-try.___ Don't know much a-bout___ al-ge-bra.___

(What a) Wonderful World - 4 - 1

© 1959 (Renewed) ABKCO MUSIC, INC., 85 Fifth Avenue, New York, NY 10003
All Rights Reserved

E
F♯
B
Don't know much a - bout the French I took.
Don't know what a slide rule is for.
But I do know that
But I do know one and
E
B
E
I love you;
one is two;
and I know that if you love me too, what a
and if this one could be with you, what a
To Coda
1.
2.
F♯
B
B
won - der - ful world this would be.
won - der - ful world this would
be. Now,
Bridge:
F♯
B
F♯
I don't claim to be an A stu - dent;
but I'm try'n' to

B
C♯7
be, for may - be by be - ing an
B
C♯7
F♯7
D.S. 𝄋 al Coda
A stu - dent, ba - by, I can win your love for me.
Coda
B
3
La ta ta ta ta ta ta,
G♯m
4
E
mm.
(His - to - ry.) (Bi -

F♯
B
G♯m
Whoa, la ta ta ta ta ta ta ta ta, mm,
ol - o - gy.)
(Sci - ence book.)
E
F♯
B
yeah. But I do know that
(French I took.)
E
B
E
I love you; and I know that if you love me too, what a
F♯
B
F♯7
B
won - der - ful world this would be.

WHAT A WONDERFUL WORLD

Words and Music by
GEORGE DAVID WEISS and BOB THIELE

C11 C7 F F+ Bbmaj7 C7
What a won - der - ful world. I see
F Am Bb Am Gm7 F
skies of blue and clouds of white, the bright bles - sed day, the
A7 Dm Db
dark sac - red night, and I think to my - self
C11 C7 F Bb F
What a won - der - ful world. The

C7
F
col - ors of the rain - bow, so pret - ty in the sky are
C7
F
al - so on the fac - es of peo - ple go - in' by, I see
Dm
C/E
Dm/F
C/G
friends shak - in' hands, say - in', "How do you do!"
3
Dm/F
F#dim
Gm7
F#dim
C7
They're real - ly say - in' "I love you," I hear
f

F Am Bb Am Gm7 F
babies cry, I watch them grow They'll learn much more than
simile
A7 Dm Db C11 C7
I'll ever know and I think to myself What a wonderful
F Am7-5 D7 Gm7
Rubato
world. Yes, I think to myself
C7-9 Slowly F Bb6 F
What a wonderful world.
rit.

WHAT'D I SAY

Words and Music by
RAY CHARLES

Bright R&B ♩ = 176

What'd I Say - 12 - 2

What'd I Say - 12 - 3

Verses 1–4:

1. Hey, ma-ma, don't you treat me wrong. Come and love your dad-dy all night long. All right now, hey, hey, all right.

2.– 4. *See additional lyrics*

What'd I Say - 12 - 4

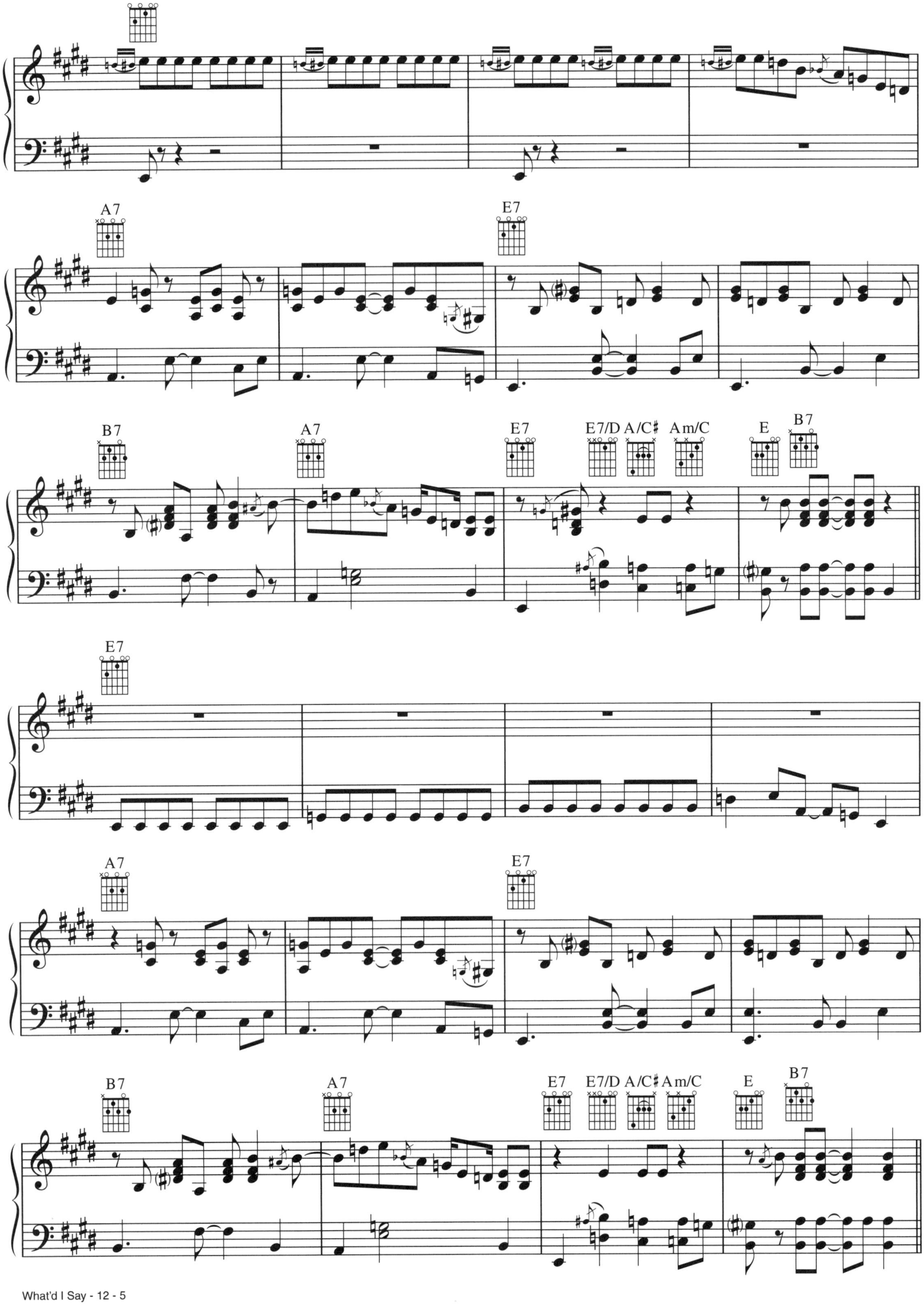
E7
A7
E7
B7
A7
E7
E7/D
A/C♯
Am/C
E
B7
E7
A7
E7
B7
A7
E7
E7/D
A/C♯
Am/C
E
B7

Verses 5 & 6:

E7
5. When you see me in mis - er - y,
6. See additional lyrics
come on, ba - by,
A7
see a - bout me, now.
Hey,
E7
hey,
B7
all right.
A7
1.
E7 E7/D A/C♯ Am/C E B7
2.
E7 E7/D A/C♯ Am/C
Well,

Chorus 1:

tell me, what'd I say? _____ Tell me, what'd I say _____

_____ right now? Tell me, what'd I say? _____

Tell me, what'd I say _____ right now? Tell me, what'd I say? _____

Tell me, what'd I say? _____ And _____ I _____ wan-na know.

Said a - I wan - na know right now.
A7
And a - I wan - na know.
Said a - I wan - na know
E7
B7
right now, yeah.
And a - I wan - na know.
A7
E7
Said a - I wan - na know, yeah.

Chorus 2–4:
N.C.
Uh,
(uh,
)
oh,
(oh,
)
uh, (uh,) oh, (oh,) uh, (uh,) oh, (oh.)
2. Oh, one more time.
3.4. See additional lyrics
E7
(Just one more time.) Said a - one more time right now.
(Just one more time.
A7
Said a - one more time now.
)
(Just one more time.)
Said a - one more time,

E7
B7
yeah.
Said a - one more time.
(Just one more time.
(Just one more time.)
A7
1.2.
E7
) Said a - one more time,
yeah.
(Just one more time.)
3.
E7
Chorus 5:
Wah!
5. Shake that thing now.
(Ba - by, it's all right.)
(Ba - by, shake that thing.
Ba - by, shake that thing now, now.
Ba - by, shake that thing.
)
(Ba - by, shake that thing.)

A7
E7
(Ba - by, shake that thing.) Ba - by, shake that thing right now.
(Ba - by, shake that thing.
B7
A7
Ba - by, shake that thing. (Ba - by, shake that thing.) Ba - by, shake that thing.
)
E7
Chorus 6:
Whoa ow! 6. Feel all right now, yeah.
(Ba - by, shake that thing.) (Ba - by, feel all right.
A7
Said I feel all right now. Oh, yeah,
) (Ba-by, feel all right.) (Ba-by, feel all right.

Verse 2:
You see the girl with the diamond ring?
She knows how to shake that thing.
All right now, hey, hey, hey, hey.

Verse 3:
Tell your mama, tell your pa,
I'm gonna send you back to Arkansas,
Oh yes, ma'am.
You don't do right, don't do right.

Verse 4:
When you see me in misery,
Come on, baby, see about me now, yeah.
All right, all right.

Verse 6:
See the girl with the red dress on?
She can do the Birdland all night long, yeah, yeah.
What'd I say? All right.
(To Chorus:)

Chorus 3:
Oh, make me feel so good. (Make me feel so good.)
Make me feel so good now, yeah. (Make me feel so good.)
Oh, baby. (Make me feel so good.)
Make me feel so good. (Make me feel so good.)
Make me feel so good, yeah. (Make me feel so good.)

Chorus 4:
Oh, it's all right. (Baby, it's all right.)
Said a-it's all right, right now. (Baby, it's all right.)
Said a-it's all right. (Baby, it's all right.)
Said a-it's all right, yeah. (Baby, it's all right.)
Said a-it's all right. (Baby, it's all right.)
Said a-it's all right. (Baby, it's all right.)
(To Chorus 5:)

WHEN A MAN LOVES A WOMAN

Words and Music by
CALVIN LEWIS and ANDREW WRIGHT

Moderately slow ♩. = 66

1. When a man____ loves a wom-an, can't keep his mind on noth-in' else.____
2. When a man____ loves a wom-an, spend__ his ver-y last____ dime____

He'd trade the world for a good thing he's found.____ If she is
try'n' to hold on to__ what he__ needs.____ He'd give up

© 1966 (Renewed) PRONTO MUSIC, MIJAC MUSIC and QUINVY MUSIC PUBLISHING CO.
All Rights on behalf of itself and MIJAC MUSIC Administered by PRONTO MUSIC, INC.
All Rights for QUINVY MUSIC PUBLISHING CO. Administered by WARNER-TAMERLANE PUBLISHING CORP.
All Rights Reserved

When a Man Loves a Woman - 4 - 1

D♭ A♭/C B♭m D♭/A♭
bad he can't see it. She can do no wrong, no.
all his com - forts and sleep out in the rain
G♭ A♭ 1. D♭ A♭
Turn his back on his best friend if he put her down. 2. When a
if she said that's the way it ought to
2. D♭ Bridge: G♭
be. When a man loves a
D♭ G♭
wom - an, I give you ev - 'ry - thing I've

D♭
G♭
got, yeah.
Try'n' to hold on to
D♭
B♭m
E♭
your precious love.
Baby, please don't treat me
Verses 3 & 4:
A♭
D♭
A♭/C
bad.
3. When a
man loves a woman
man loves a woman,
B♭m
D♭/A♭
G♭
A♭
down deep in his soul,
he can do her no wrong.
she can bring him such miser-
He can never own some other

D♭ A♭ D♭ A♭/C
y.___ If she is play - ing him for a fool,
girl.___ Yes, when a man___ loves a wom - an,
B♭m D♭/A♭ G♭ A♭
he's the last one to know.___ Lov - ing eyes can___ nev - er
I know ex - act - ly how he feels,___ 'cause, ba - by, ba - by, you're my
1. D♭ A♭ 2. D♭ A♭ D♭ A♭/C
see. 4. When a world. When a man___ loves a wom - an.
Repeat ad lib. and fade
B♭m A♭6 G♭ A♭7 D♭ A♭
When a

WIPE OUT

By
THE SURFARIS

Brightly, with a beat

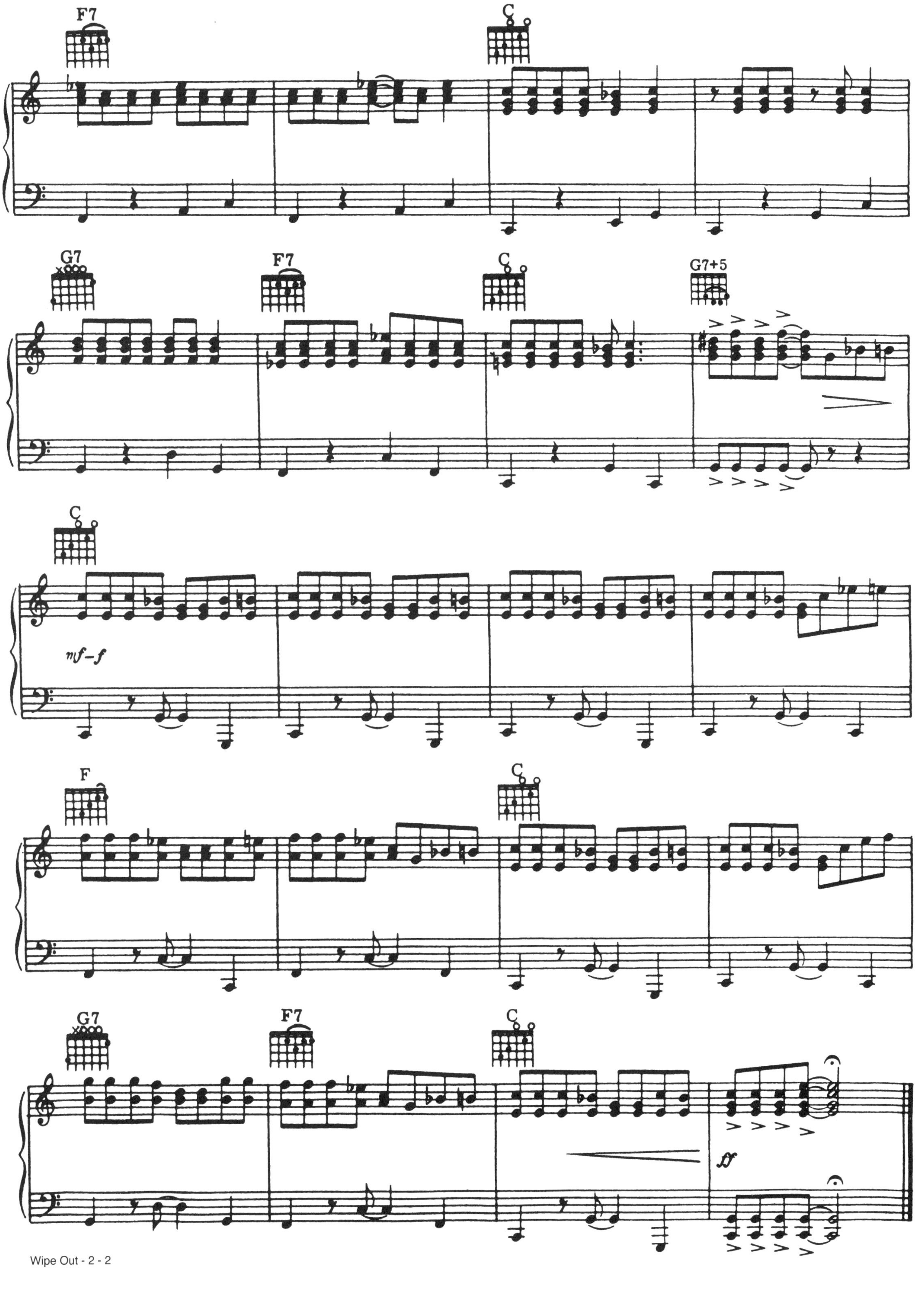
F7
C
G7
F7
C
G7+5
C
mf–f
F
C
G7
F7
C
ff

YOU CAN'T ALWAYS GET WHAT YOU WANT

Guitar in Open E tuning *(optional w/ Capo at 8th fret)*:
⑥ = E   ③ = G♯
⑤ = B   ② = B
④ = E   ① = E

Words and Music by
MICK JAGGER and
KEITH RICHARDS

Moderately ♩ = 104

(Boys Choir) I saw her to-day at the re-cep-tion, a glass of wine in her hand. I know she would meet her con-nec-tion, at her feet was a foot-loose man. No, you can't al-ways get what you want. You can't al-ways get what you

(Choir) Aah, aah, aah, aah. Aah, aah, aah, aah. Aah, aah, aah,

You Can't Always Get What You Want - 10 - 1

© 1969 (Renewed) ABKCO MUSIC, INC., 85 Fifth Avenue, New York, NY 10003
All Rights Reserved

want. You can't al - ways get what you want. And if you
aah. Aah, aah,
try some time you'll find you get what you need.
aah, aah, aah.
F
C
(Guitar)
mp
C2
C
C2
C
C2
C
C2
C
F
(French Horn)
C2
* (Cont. chord pattern throughout)
F
C2

(Lead Vocal) 1. I saw her to-day at the re-cep-tion,

5. *See additional lyrics*

a glass of wine in her hand. I knew she was gon-na meet her con-nec-tion. At her feet was a foot - loose man. You

Chorus:

can't al - ways get what you want. You

can't al - ways get what you want. You

To Coda

can't al - ways get what you want. But if you

try some-times,___ well, you might find___ you get what you need._ Oh, yeah.___

Verses 2, 3, & 4:

___ down___ to the___ dem-on-stra-tion___ to get___
3. 4. *See additional lyrics*

___ my___ fair share___ of a-buse.___ Sing-in', "We're___

225

gon - na vent our frus - tra - tion. If we don't, we're gon - na blow a fif - ty - amp fuse." Sing it to me, now. You

1. 3. To Next Strain

2.

4. We de - cid - can't al - ways get what you want.

Chorus:

You can't al - ways get what you want.

F7
C7
F7
You can't al - ways get what you want.
But if you
D
F
try some - times,
well, you just might find,
you get what you
1.
C7
F7
C7
need.
Oh
ba - by,
yeah.
F7
2.
C7
F7
3. I
need.
Oh,
yeah.
Whoo!

D7sus/A
D7sus/B
D7sus/C
(Choir)
Aah,
aah,
D7sus
D7sus/G
aah,
aah.
Chorus:
C7
F7
C7
Aah,
aah,
aah,
F7
C7
F7
aah,
aah,
aah.

D
10
F
8
C7
8
You get what you need.
F7
8
C7
8
F7
8
D.S. al Coda
5. I
Coda
D
10
F
8
try some - time, you just might find, you just might find you get what you
C7
8
F7
8
need.
(Choir) Aah,
aah,

Verse 3:
I went down to the Chelsea drugstore
To get your prescription filled.
I was standin' in line with Mr. Jimmy.
A-man, did he look pretty ill.

Verse 4:
We decided that we would have a soda;
My favorite flavor, cherry red,
I sung my song to Mr. Jimmy.
Yeah, and he said one word to me, and that was "dead."
I said to him…
(To Chorus:)

Verse 5:
I saw her today at the reception.
In her glass was a bleeding man.
She was practiced at the art of deception.
Well, I could tell by her blood-stained hands.
Say it!
(To Chorus:)

YOU DON'T HAVE TO SAY YOU LOVE ME

(Io Che Non Vivo [Senza Te])

English Lyrics by
VICKI WICKHAM and SIMON NAPIER-BELL
Original Italian Lyrics by V. PALLAVICINI

Music by
PINO DONAGGIO

now you've gone a-way. Don't you see that now you've gone and I'm left here on my own; that I have to fol-low you and

Gm7(♭5)
C7
beg you to come home.
Chorus:
F
Dm
Gm
C7
You don't have to say you love me, just be close at hand.
mf
F
Dm
Gm7
C7
You don't have to stay for - ev - er, I will un - der - stand. Be -
F
Am
Dm
lieve me, be - lieve me, I can't help but love you. But be -

lieve me, I'll nev-er tie you down.

Verse 2:
2. Left a-lone with just a mem-o-ry, life seems dead and quite un-real. All that's left is lone-li-ness, there's

234

Chorus:

You don't have to say you love me, just be close at hand.

You don't have to stay for-ev-er, I will un-der-stand, be-

lieve me, be-lieve me.

You Don't Have to Say You Love Me - 6 - 5

Chorus:
G Em Am D7
You don't have to say you love me, just be close at hand.
G Em Am7 D7
You don't have to stay for - ev - er, I will un - der - stand, be -
G Dm6 G Dm6
lieve me, be - lieve me, be -
poco cresc.
G
lieve me.

A WHITER SHADE OF PALE

Words and Music by
KEITH REID and GARY BROOKER

Moderately slow ♩ = 76

F
Am/E
Dm
F/C
turned cart - wheels 'cross the floor;
and the truth is plain to see."
G
G/F
Em
G7
I was feel - ing kind of sea - sick,
But I wan - dered through my play - ing cards
C
Em/B
Am
C/G
the crowd called out for more.
and would not let her be
F
Am/E
Dm
F/C
The room was hum - ming hard - er
one of six - teen ves - tal vir - gins

as the ceil - ing flew a - way.
who were leav - ing for the coast.

When we called out for an - oth - er drink,
And al-though my eyes were o - pen,

the wait - er brought a tray.
they might just as well been closed. And so it

Chorus:

was_____ that lat - er,

F
Am/E
Dm
F/C
as the mill - er told his tale,
G
G/F
Em
G7
that her face, at first just ghost - ly, turned a
C
F
1.
C
G7
whit - er shade of pale.
2.
C
G7
Interlude:
C
Em/B
pale.

And so it

A Whiter Shade of Pale - 5 - 5

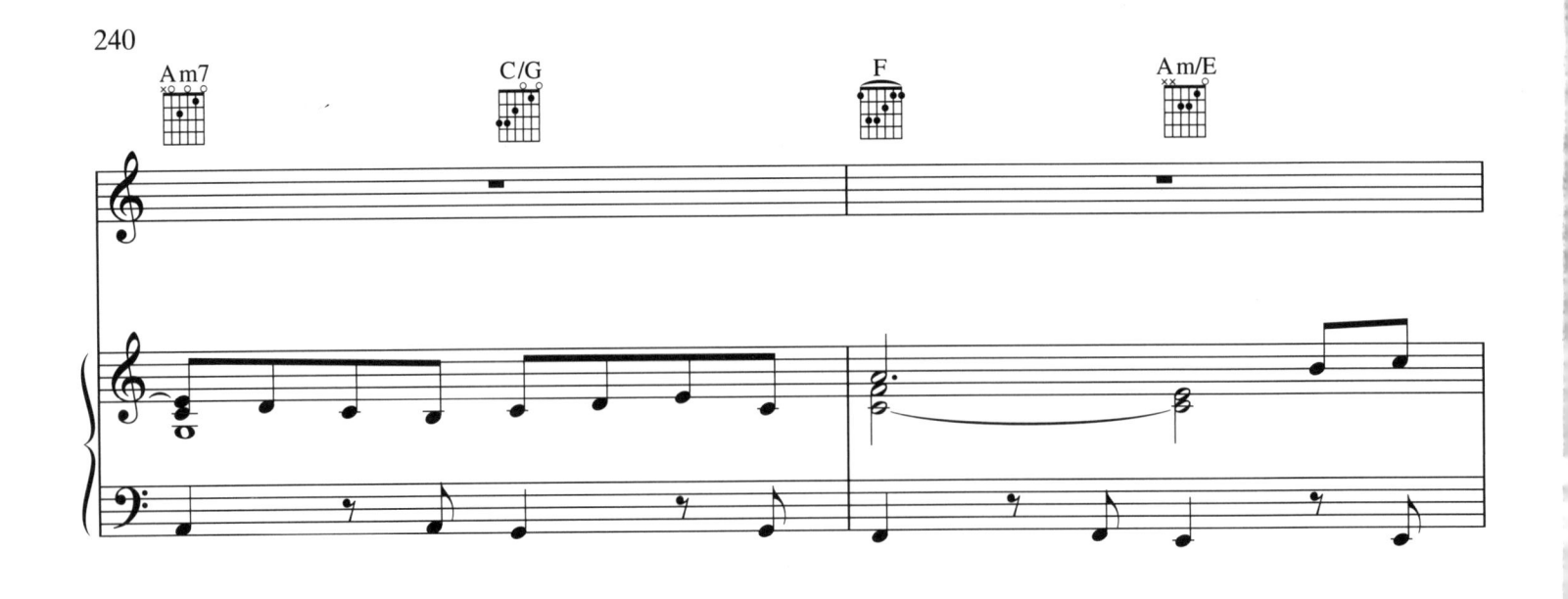

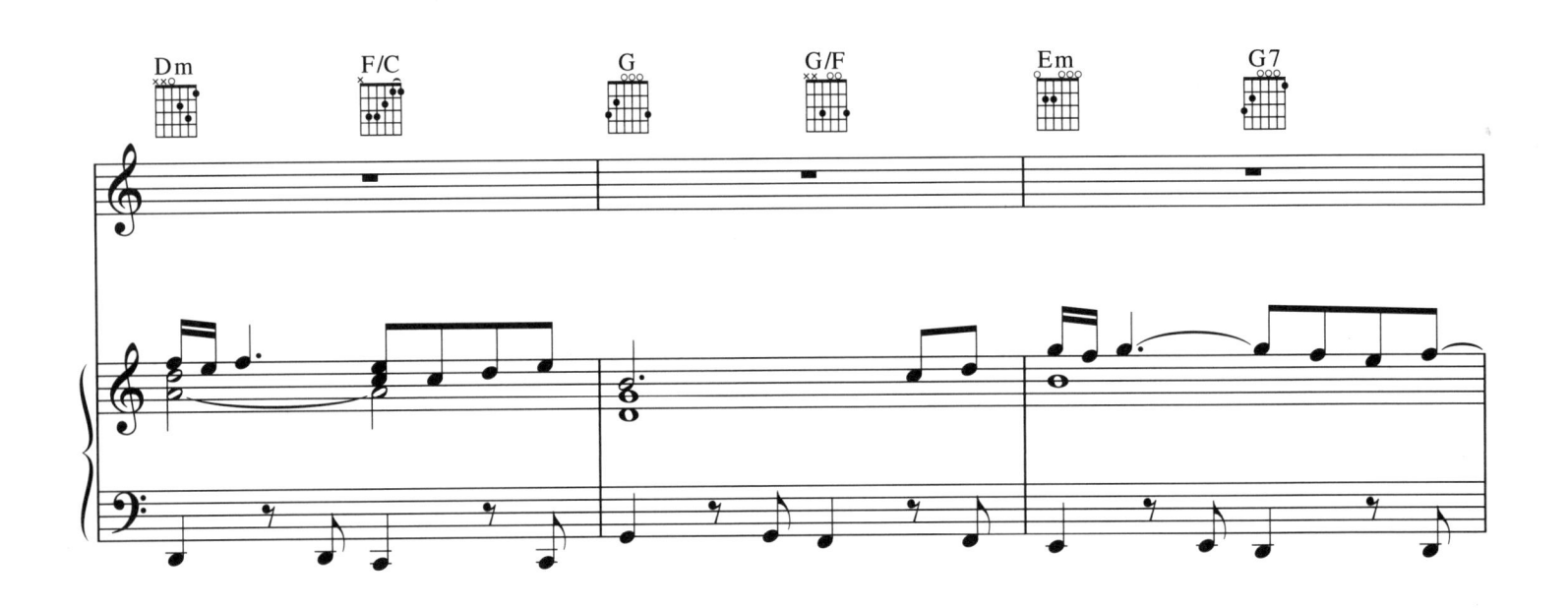